The Coming Deflation

The Coming Deflation

ITS DANGERS – AND OPPORTUNITIES

C. V. MYERS

ARLINGTON HOUSE·PUBLISHERS
NEW ROCHELLE, NEW YORK

TO MURIEL

Eighth Printing, August 1977
Copyright © 1976 C. V. Myers

Manufactured in the United States of America

Library of Congress Cataloging in Publication
Data
Myers, C   V
  The coming deflation.
  Includes index.
  1. Deflation (Finance)—United
  States. 2. Currency
question—United States. I. Title.
HG538.M93   332.4'1'0973   75-46514
ISBN 0-87000-356-9

CONTENTS

FOREWORD

History is made up of tidal movements. They are not recognizable as such while they are going on; only in retrospect do they become discernible. Thus we speak of the Age of the Pyramids and the Glory of Egypt. Even further back we recognize the Stone Age and the Bronze Age. We see the Grecian Age of enlightenment, the age of the Roman Empire, the Middle Ages, the Industrial Revolution.

Within the ages there are eras. These eras are extended periods of certain prevailing ideas. The time of the Crusades was such an era. It was fashionable for staunch Christians to teach the infidel Turks what they had better believe.

There was the era of expansion of mighty empires. Nations sought to acquire lands in all corners of the earth, and to exploit them, and to bring them under the central flag. This practice was quite acceptable. The era of imperialism persisted right into the twentieth century.

But while these eras were in progress, they were hardly recognizable. Probably no newspaper wrote about the Industrial Revolution as it was progressing. Only later do we see that it represented, indeed, a revolutionary change in the mode of human existence on the earth.

Less talked about is the era of the gold standard, where for nearly 200 years the British pound was absolutely as good as gold and could be freely exchanged for gold by anyone at any time. The real gold stood behind the pound. It was the era of the greatest monetary stability and progress in the history of the world to that time.

World War I marked the beginning of the **era of credit** on a massive scale. The world was prosperous. Savings were large. All that was needed to get the money to fight the war was to **borrow** on these holdings. Owners were issued certificates—called bonds—that were simply a promise to pay back the real wealth that was being borrowed. Because these bonds were believed to be as good as money, and the money as good as gold, they were transferable at face value from person to person, or country to country.

This massive debt, however, came to roost in the late twenties when it was discovered that the real wealth represented by the bonds could not be paid back in full. Britain had to back away from the gold standard. The inflation of that period reduced the value of the debt and was a partial repudiation of the debt.

During World War II the same process was repeated on a vastly larger scale. Moreover, the accumulation of debt did not end with the war; it accelerated as the winners and losers alike undertook to rebuild the horrendous destruction.

Instead of paying off the debts accumulated by the fruitless efforts of war, governments had to rebuild; and they wanted to expand; so they borrowed more, issued more bonds. Debt piled on debt. There is no limit to debt, except a limit of confidence.

As long as the instrument of debt—printed money or bonds—continues to be accepted at face value, it can be circulated from person to person and country to country. When there is no longer enough private money to buy more bonds, governments simply issue new ones. And these circulate—just as counterfeit money would—along with the old bonds that represented real money or, in other words, real commodities or articles or service of real value. Quite unwittingly we were moving into a NEW ERA. It was the era of inflation. So great was the confidence of the brave new world that it seemed as if this could go on forever. The following line of thought became fashionable: What does it matter what we owe? Business is good. We owe this debt to ourselves. And as long as we have growth and prosperity, who cares about what figures are on the paper?

This type of thinking remained popular over such a protracted period of time that it truly amounted to a new era.

It was downright unpopular to suggest that someday these debts might have to be paid off. That would take the money out of the banking system—because when a debt is paid off, that amount of money, originally issued simply by a book entry, is canceled out. That would have reduced the money supply, causing a contraction of business. The answer was that, if debts had to be paid off—just print more money to pay them. No one seemed to bother to ask, who would **buy** the new debts. And even if someone would buy, what would he buy with, since nearly all of the real wealth had already been used as an instrument of credit.

The politicians and the money-makers remained undaunted. If there were no buyers for the new instruments of credit, they would simply create the new instruments—which they did.

And herein lay the seed of the collapse of the era of inflation. Because when all the real wealth had been gathered together and committed, the new wealth could do no more than water it down. We had a gallon of real whisky. When there was no more real whisky to add, the governments and moneymen added water. For a long time the watered-down whisky was passed off as real whisky. As long as no one tasted it, or demanded an analysis, it worked just as well as the real whisky. So now we had two gallons of whisky and later, because we were getting into trouble with wages and costs, we added another gallon of water. Now we had three gallons, but really, still, only one gallon of whisky.

By 1975 this process had continued to the point where we had five gallons of money, which was really worth only one gallon. Almost without exception, everything needed by human beings had increased in price between four and five times. A nickel cup of coffee was now worth 20 cents. A $1,000 car of three decades ago was now worth $4,000; a $10,000 home of 1940 was now worth $40,000 to $50,000. We had simply watered down the whisky.

Without knowing it we had, because of World War II, entered into a new era—a third of a century of inflation.

The was not the first time that the human race, having become prosperous, had overextended itself and imagined that prosperity was a God-given and eternal right. It had happened with Genghis Khan. It had happened with Babylon. It had happened with Rome. It had happened with France. It had happened with Germany. The result was, without exception, consistently, identically, and unalterably the same— collapse of money as a medium of exchange.

The new era, this latest era of inflation, differed from the others in two important aspects. Firstly, it was massive—worldwide—and on a scale never before dreamed of. This was possible because of the invention of the credit mechanism of bonds, IOU's of various types, made prevalent in the U.S. by the Federal Reserve System that had been empowered to create money simply by book entry; and by the use of the Gold Exchange Standard that virtually doubled the amount of credit previously available for one ounce of gold.

All of this tended to conceal the unbelievable mass of credit.

The second difference was the vastly improved means of communication and, therefore, of propaganda. As long as the newspapers believed that the process of inflation could continue without disaster, there was a good chance the public would believe it, especially when there never seemed to be any penalty for the accumulation of credit. The magician can make you believe that he has ten rabbits instead of one, as long as you don't demand actual delivery of the rabbits. And so we had the invention of Special Drawing Rights—or, as it was so inanely named, "paper gold."

The name itself would have been enough to alert a man out of the Bronze Age to the suspicion that something was fishy. But with all of the economists and the highest monetary authorities believing in the fantasy, and propagating the fantasy through the public press, the population, still eating beefsteak and driving big cars, began to believe in the fantasy too. Money need not be anything. As long as the proper figures were written down in the proper book, money at the central bank level was unlimited.

Historians in future years will find it hard to believe that supposedly sane adult people could fall for such a crazy scheme. But humanity moves in waves of fashion. And when it is fashionable to believe that paper is in every respect substitutable for gold, then you will be very unpopular if you should take the opposite view, even if you try to prove it by setting the two substances side by side. They will call you unenlightened—you just haven't caught up with modern times.

The point of this book is that we have, indeed, been swept up in an era of inflation; and secondly, that this era is in a terminal condition; and thirdly, that the inevitable result of the termination of vast inflation is collapse; and fourthly, to try to determine what we shall face in this era of collapse; and fifthly, to plan as well as we can to withstand the enormous social dislocations that will accompany the collapse of money.

The vastness of the changes facing our civilization and our mode of life will tax your imagination before you have finished.

1

PRECIPITATION WITHOUT WARNING

A book about money—if it is to be worth a reader's time—must be of practical value. Few are interested in the theories on money or the academic considerations that so fascinate the professors and the vast congregation of economists who formulate economic policy.

Unfortunately, it will be hard if not impossible for you to accept the practical conclusions that I shall draw *unless,* first of all, you are led to understand the fundamentals that are the very bedrock of the economy, and therefore of money; and therefore of the social structure of our country, and thus the world.

Almost anyone could see by reading the newspapers in 1974 and 1975 that we were building up to some kind of drastic adjustment. The bulk of the population had faith that the planners in the backrooms had the situation well in hand and were already planning to implement the blueprints that would set us back on an even keel. But I have news for you. The planners have no idea how to restore equilibrium to the international monetary situation, and therefore to the various western economies. Contrary to what you may be led to believe by inference, these men are stumbling forward one step at a time, hoping against hope that some as yet unforeseen development will take place to extricate them from a deepening morass. They have no idea what to do next.

Therein lies the cause for alarm. Therein lies the reason why you must, if you intend to survive financially, *understand* first of all the conditions that have brought us to the brink of a monetary collapse.

Moreover, there is an urgency to this situation.

You may remember from your early chemistry that if you were adding a solution of weak hydrochloric acid to a strong solution of sodium hydroxide, you could continue to add bit by bit without marking any noticeable change. It would be very easy to think the process could go on forever. But sooner or later there came a critical point. When that critical point arrived, suddenly the solution changed. The clear liquid was now a cloudy mass. The precipitation had taken place instantly.

Inflation in the economic system is like adding a weak solution of hydrochloric acid. Its early introduction results in no visible difference. The process can be continued by degrees to the point where the whole population begins to accept inflation with complacence. After all, it hasn't wrecked us yet, why should we think it's going to later on? Why not learn to live with it?

This became the generally accepted attitude through the late sixties and early seventies. We must learn to live with inflation.

But by 1974 a keen observer could see that we must be reaching the point of saturation, and therefore nearing the point of precipitation. With interest rates above 12 percent, how could building go on? How could a wage earner expect to pay off a home, a car, and all of the other so-called necessities? How could business expect to expand without continually higher prices?

The stock market had been in decline since 1966. Although it still stood at 850 in 1974, compared with 1000 in 1966, few people stopped to consider that inflation during that period had amounted to more than one-third and that, therefore, the 850 level of the Dow Jones was actually more like 650. When D.J. hit 580 in late 1974, its real value was more like 380 compared with the value of 1000 in early 1966. The quoted value of the stocks on the New York Stock Exchange had depreciated two-thirds in real value! During eight years of inflation and continually higher prices and continually higher wages, we had, nevertheless, been sinking deeper in an inexorable downtrend. But the stockbrokers, with their noses deep in detail, didn't recognize it. The public didn't recognize it. That's why it hasn't precipitated yet.

Well, what if it should precipitate? As a reader you want to know. And you'd better know it. Here is what happens:

When the weak solution of inflation has been added to the economy to the critical point of precipitation—the whole solution changes. We have a stormy cloud of falling particles. We have the precipitation of credit.

When the interest rates get high enough, the borrowers have to scamper to borrow more to serve the interest on their debts. But in this era of credit and inflation there are many more borrowers than there are creditors. The debt load is enormously larger than the assets. Corporations in America owe 90 cents on every dollar of assets. But with the spiraling interest rates, the servicing of a debt of 90 percent threatens to destroy the asset.

There are several signs that precipitation is imminent. In 1971 we had the bankruptcy of Lockheed, which nearly triggered the bankruptcy of the Bank of America. The situation was only saved by an act of Congress. The government of the country had to use taxpayer money to hold one corporation from going bankrupt. Then we had the Penn Central, the largest corporation of its kind in the world. Again the same remedy. In 1974 we had a severe warning when the Franklin National Bank, one of the largest in the United States, had to call on the Federal Reserve System to keep it solvent. The frightening thing about the event was that the news was allowed to get out at all. Normally banks will pitch in to save another bank in order to maintain confidence in the banking system. The banks of the United States either were unwilling or unable to assist Franklin. The Federal Reserve had to do it.

Indeed, there were indications that we were reaching the critical level of concentration of inflation.

Now, after your solution of hydrochloric acid has reached the stage of precipitation, it will not matter how much more hydrochloric acid you use. You can pour in five gallons. It will have no effect on the chemical solution, or on the precipitation. Once the solution has been precipitated, it cannot be unprecipitated by the addition of the hydrochloric acid.

Once inflation has precipitated the credit structure, no amount of additional inflation can bring it back. It can be poured in till hell freezes over. When credit has collapsed, no amount of inflation can restore it.

The end product of the precipitation of credit is *deflation.*

Simply expressed, deflation means letting the air out of the balloon. We get back to the things that are real. We get back to values that are real. We find that the prices prior to the precipitation were far too high. So now we are back at lower prices. That means that the money we have —if we have been fortunate to hang on to money—will now buy much more than it would before the period of precipitation. The precipitation of credit has caused bankruptcies far and wide. This has reduced the money supply. It has reduced the money in circulation so drastically that all of the goods and services combined are worth much less in numbers of dollars than they were prior to the precipitation.

This is bad news for any creditor. It is bad news for the overextended banks of America. It is bad news for the heavily stock-invested pension funds. It is bad news for debtors who may be called to pay, because unless then can pay they will find that they have become a part of the precipitation, which is bankruptcy.

During late 1974 and 1975 the chorus of those predicting continuing inflation was becoming louder and louder. The only hope for avoiding precipitation was the hope that the critical concentration was still a long way off. If everyone would believe that, perhaps confidence could be retained so that indeed the critical level could be further delayed.

But history tells us there is inevitably and always a critical level to inflation—a level at which precipitation of credit occurs. You don't know where it is. I don't know where it is. But one thing you may know for certain: when it comes you will be living in a different solution. You will be living in a new economic climate. In short, the environment in which you have thrived for 40 years will suddenly have been transformed. The era of inflation and debt will have disappeared. You will be facing new circumstances. Some will be ready; most will not.

I could go on right here and tell you what I think you should do to meet this new environment. But that would only have the thrust of empirical statements by one man. Why should you accept such empirical statements? Even if you did, would you have confidence you had done the right thing?

Alas, there is only one way for you to arrive at the fundamental conclusions that, hopefully, will preserve your wealth and your substance. That is through your own understanding. That means that you will have to understand how the conclusions are arrived at, and why they are unavoidable and inevitable. Before you can benefit from anyone's suggestions, these suggestions must have been mentally digested by you, and thus have become a part of your own mentality. Then, and then only, will you be in a position to act with confidence and—once those actions have been taken—to rest at peace.

The energy crisis has brought the American population up short. Within a few months inflation had precipitated a worldwide energy dilemma. Most people still don't realize that the cause of this energy crisis was inflation; that the oil-producing nations had found out that the store of value they kept in the ground was being depreciated quickly on the surface once they had turned it into dollars. As long as they kept it in the ground it retained its value. Once it was pumped above ground it lost value. As long as they didn't need the cash, it didn't make sense to produce the oil except at twice the price.

But no news announcement from Washington ever bothered to explain that the depreciating U.S. dollar was the direct cause of the energy crisis. And that, further, the high price of oil means a higher cost of living—and that, further, the higher cost of living means a reduced living standard for all people of the United States, unless somehow the United States can inherently produce more with which to pay for the raw materials from abroad—and that, further, a contraction in the standard of living, with the attendant reduction in spending and borrowing, can only mean unemployment and lower profits for corporations— and that, further, such conditions will precipitate the calling of loans— and that, further, people who are desperate to pay their loans to avoid bankruptcy will promise to pay interest rates of 12 percent—and that, further, this process at a point nearby reaches the critical level of concentration—and that, further, the inevitable end is a monstrous depression.

This book tells about the ending of one era and the beginning of another. The whole social system is going to turn over in the next decade; the guideposts of the last 40 years will be discarded; new guideposts will arise in their place; and, as a result of all this, our society will be transformed.

Please read on about money; and when it is all over, let us get together at the end of the book and try to figure out what each individual may do to save himself.

2

THE NATURE OF MONEY

Money is stored-up labor—the fruit of sweat, put into cold storage. But if it deteriorates in storage, who is going to save it? If you could only be paid off in tomatoes, would you bother to work in order to save? A collapsed currency is rotted storage.

The collapse of a currency is not a new event in world history. It has happened countless times. When a currency collapses it ceases to operate as a medium of exchange, and trade reverts to barter.

Unremitting inflation of a currency has resulted invariably, inevitably, monotonously, and without exception in the collapse of the currency.

It's strange that a cause-and-effect relationship as old as Babylon, one that has never varied, could be so repeatedly challenged—that presumably intelligent men could be led to believe that they somehow had stumbled on a method that could make a fool of natural law.

Universal and natural laws are well known to the human race—from the peasant to the king. The king knows that if he drops a stone from between his fingers it will always go down. It will never go up. It will never go sideways. The peasant knows this equally well. There has never been an exception to this law in all of the history of intelligent behavior on this earth. Man's existence on earth is a phenomenon of nature.

Economics is the foundation of civilized existence. Therefore economics operates by natural law.

All natural laws are simple, and without exception immutable. They *never* change. You cannot consume more than you produce, unless you (a) take something away from someone else, or (b) unless you get him to lend it to you. But then you must pay it back. If you do not pay it back, you have either confiscated it, or you have *tricked* him into turning over to you—without compensation—that which was his. In any case, the excess of your consumption over your production has been at the expense of another man, who consequently had to consume less.

This brings us to examine the very foundation of society. At the root of any kind of social organization stands this dictum: *No man may be permitted to take by force what belongs to another man.* In other words, *Thou shalt not steal.*

Without this cornerstone of human conduct—without this prohibition—there could be no society whatsoever. Not even a tribe. Bandits would plunder the countryside, and then plunder one another. Ten—not even two—people could not cooperate to build a shelter—because, when it was finished, the stronger would take the shelter for himself and turn the weaker one out to perish in the storm.

So, underlying the structure of society is the recognition of private property—the inalienable right of a man to keep what is his even though he may not have the physical strength to defend this right.

As society developed, men willingly submitted to certain restraints in order to make life better for all. They agreed that any of their members violating this cardinal rule would be punished. Not too long ago the cattle owners of the West collectively hanged rustlers from the branches of trees for the violation of this law of private property.

Without this law, liberty and prosperity are impossible because every man would live in fear that the fruit of his effort would be taken from him. Also he would only exert effort to obtain essentials from day to day. To try to accumulate a *store of value* would be pointless.

From this, then, we may say: You can only consume more than you produce at the expense of someone else; and if you do that—when you are discovered—you will be punished.

In other words, consumption in excess of production will always result in a penalty for someone. This is true for a person, true for a tribe, and true for a country.

Thus it is clear that one country cannot, in aggregate, consume in excess of its production except with a resulting penalty to another country.

When you have said this you have said that no nation in the world can run a balance-of-payments deficit without paying it back or without the consequences of its excess consumption having been paid for by others. The question of who will absorb the penalty is the basis of the current confrontations—and the unremitting crises in the world.

From this springboard we can now clearly define the nature of money.

3

A STANDARD OF MEASURE

Man's desires to acquire goods and to hoard them beyond his present needs are unlimited. His desire to acquire the services of other humans is likewise unlimited, since such services can be used in the acquisition of further goods.

But we have seen that the acquisitiveness of man would result in anarchy unless restrained; and so man's nature in organized society finds expression in the form of trade.

He acquires a thing he wants by giving up something of his own, or by performing a service. The more he performs for others (work) the more things he can acquire. If, by a chance, he has an unusual talent, it may be that for the products of an hour of his time he can engage someone of a lesser talent for a period of two or three hours. So, in a free society, one man's productivity may be higher than the productivity of another man and, in this case, he will end up with more worldly goods and services than the other.

But how can such things as the differential productivity of two men be measured? It can only be measured in goods, in *things*. How can this exchange (barter) of goods proceed in a smooth and orderly manner? The answer is the use of a standard of measurement. And that is the first function of money—a medium of exchange.

The most reliable understanding of money is the understanding at the level of the peasant. After all, most of us are essentially peasants. The overwhelming majority of us understand only that we want to acquire goods and services, and we, within ourselves, are the sole dictators of the amount of effort we will exert in the acquisition of these wants. So, in the final analysis—regardless of all the monetary experts—the people will become the dictators of price.

To really understand money we must have the simple outlook of a peasant, a producer, a farmer, a carpenter. The more closely we think like those who sell only services (e.g., engineers and doctors) the less we comprehend. When we reach the top pinnacle of political and monetary theory, we shall have lost contact with the earthly meaning of money.

And so, in your imagination, I want you to join with me upon an adventure.

We shall suppose that we are going to form a new colony on some hospitable but uninhabited isle. There is a boatload of us, and we are taking along with us every conceivable commodity and every type of worker as a cross-section of our society. We start with all of this.

We call our country FREEDONIA.

When we have finally disembarked on the island, someone suddenly remembers that we have forgotten to bring any money. We have the price lists of everything—and a list of who owns what—but no money.

On our consignment list of property, every person has been accredited with all of the general commodities of necessity and luxury. For example, everyone has in the storehouse an ownership of three cans of pipe tobacco, although many do not smoke. Everyone has two bottles of perfume. I have soon smoked up my pipe tobacco, and I ask my wife what am I going to do. She replies that Jack Jones, who likes candy, ran out of candy, and he worked for several hours for Mr. Smith who was building a sunporch and who did not like candy, and got, in exchange, candy from Smith. Perhaps I can do the same for pipe tobacco.

I say no, I do not want to work for Smith; I will trade my accredited perfume with Mrs. Doe for pipe tobacco that she does not use. When I go to Mrs. Doe she does not want to trade with me because she does not want any more perfume, but she does love canned peaches. We have eaten our canned peaches. So now I must hunt for someone else who does not care for canned peaches but who likes perfume. I must trade my perfume for the canned peaches, which then I, in turn, take to Mrs. Doe and offer for the pipe tobacco.

This is barter. This is the way primitive trade took place. It was cumbersome, and organized society advanced slowly under the system of barter. An immense amount of effort was wasted in matching the customers of trade. It's obvious that our new colony will not function very smoothly under this system, although we have collectively all the goods that we need.

The elected leaders confer. Someone says that since we have all the prices and the values and a complete inventory of all the materials, we will manufacture our own money to the exact extent of the materials we have. We will make this in denominations large and small to accommodate any size of purchase. All of the materials will be placed together in a storehouse, and taken from the ownership of all the people. All of the people will be given their credit (money) to the extent of their ownership in these materials.

Now I do not have to search out Mrs. Doe at all. I can go to the storehouse and for the prescribed amount of money I can immediately purchase my tobacco.

The leaders have also decided that since money could be so easily lost or misplaced, a clearing house for money itself would be in order. All or any of us may place the money we have received into our accounts in this clearing house or bank.

We have made a terrific stride forward. All of the time and effort expended in the search to match buyers and sellers can now be applied to production. We can use this time to build more shelters or swings or umbrellas or whatnot—greatly improving our comfort and, therefore, our standard of living. This plan seems to be working out very well.

After a while we find that we have assets—things—commodities we have grown in the garden—beyond the original amount of money collectively deposited in this bank, and we are being hampered in the matter of exchange because of a lack of money to match the expanded amount of goods. Prices have been going down. Either they will continue to go down as the volume of goods increases, or we shall have to have more money.

Again a meeting is called. We find prices have gone down about 10 percent. So we decide to increase the money supply by 10 percent. We have discovered that to make this colony work smoothly we shall continually have to increase the money supply as the results of our labors increase the goods.

We adopt this policy, and now we are in high gear. There is no limit to the amount of hours a man may work and produce, and thus earn more of this money with which to buy more goods that have been also produced by others. Although our money supply has increased, prices remain perfectly stable. Money is functioning smoothly as a medium of exchange.

It was the discovery of money as a medium of exchange that led to an enormous advance in civilization and to the harnessing of the power, abilities, initiative and the ingenuity of man. All of his talents were put to work to the collective benefit of all, although each man was able to retain for himself the fruits of his own labor.

Note that it was completely unnecessary for the leaders of this colony to pass a law that this money is legal tender and must be accepted as a payment of debts. Such a law would have been superfluous. Natural law is in operation. Each and all of the colonists know that all of the other colonists are anxious to acquire this money. It is not necessary to force it on anybody. It represents real goods. *It is in fact real wealth.* It is not just a symbol of wealth. It is wealth itself in a *different* and *convenient* form. Real money is a highly desired medium of exchange, and it *is* wealth.

Note too that it will not be necessary to have any laws regulating the price of items. If those who grow potatoes in their gardens grow more potatoes than the aggregate collective demands, they will not be able to sell all those potatoes. The result will be that some offer potatoes at a lower price. This brings down the price of most of the sellers of potatoes. Under these circumstances some housewives will say, "We will eat more potatoes and fewer turnips which have been in short supply this year." So the potatoes are consumed at the lower price, and the price of turnips, which had risen beyond the year before, begins to recede to the normal price. The producers of the community are responsive to these conditions and regulate their crops accordingly.

Any controls by the state or the elected representatives of our new state would be superfluous and disruptive.

This machine is operating like a dream.

Also notice we have no gold or silver. People are able to buy gold and silver jewelry in the stores, but it is not a functioning part of our monetary system. Up to this point there has been no reason to introduce gold and silver money, or any kind of backing for the money. The backing for this money is the actual commodities in use. Each piece of money is actually a warehouse receipt. There is no need for an intervening medium.

Herein lies the basis of the argument of so many people that gold is unnecessary in the functioning of a monetary system. To this point they have won the argument. But this society is not finished yet. There is much more to come. There are certain natural laws springing from human nature that have not, to this point, come into play.

4

A STORE OF VALUE

In our Freedonia, money is a highly reliable store of value. We know that the money we save today can be used tomorrow or next year to buy exactly the same value in goods as it will buy today. This is true because the money supply is kept constant with the amount of goods available. As long as this condition is maintained, we can have complete confidence in this money—even though it is only paper. For, in truth, it is much more than paper, it is the actual *warehouse receipt* of the goods *physically* existing.

Unfortunately and unknowingly we have picked up a few crooks in our excursion to this new colony. Any society contains some crooks—people who will try to acquire the assets of others, if not by force, then by subterfuge.

It has not gone unnoticed by these crooks that the printed pieces of paper money can be reproduced. With the help of some smart managers and good technicians, these crooks set up a clandestine printing press and begin to produce apparently identical money. This money finds its way into the stream of our money supply. The fake five-dollar bill will buy every bit as much as the real five-dollar bill. It is now that our system begins to malfunction.

If we had a million dollars representing the goods and services, and our crooks produce one hundred thousand dollars of bogus money that becomes intermixed with the real money, we have a money supply 10 percent in excess of our warehouse receipts. It is clear that if more money bids for the same goods, the price of the goods goes up. If ten men have one dollar to buy ten bags of flour, and if someone slips each one of them an extra dollar, the price that can be paid for the flour under competitive bidding will rise. In general this doesn't happen right away, because some of the money is placed in savings accounts, but before long we will notice a rise in prices.

The crooks have now obtained for themselves a claim on 10 percent of all of the physical goods of our colony. The loss has been suffered proportionately by all members of the colony. Without the use of force our crooks have managed to steal from us all. The result has been the same as if the goods had been taken at gunpoint. We are witnessing the beginning of the breakdown of society, the introduction of an element that, if allowed to continue, would end in anarchy comparable to the anarchy that results when the strong can pillage the weak with impunity.

This must be stopped. If it is not stopped the counterfeiters will continue to make money until they own 20 percent, 30 percent—or, eventually, all of the assets of society.

Fortunately we have some fairly smart detectives in our colony and they have observed that some of the circulating money has a tiny smudge in one corner that differentiates it from the real money. Now the society is alerted. These bogus bills are picked up as they are returned to the bank, and destroyed. That has only half solved our problem, because the goods that were bought with the bogus money are still in the hands of the as-yet-unknown crooks. The rest of the society has suffered a loss of these goods.

Finally, the clandestine printing press is discovered and these con men are brought to justice. They have stolen as clearly and indisputably as the cattle rustler has stolen. The only difference in the two crimes is the identity of the victim. Here the victim is the whole society. These counterfeiters are convicted for taking goods belonging to others. So they are herded together and hanged from trees.

The most important point we made here is that while this counterfeiting was going on the money supply had been increased over and above the value of the goods, and consequently prices had increased. We had inflation.

The introduction of this inflation was a shock to our money system. It meant that the dollar saved the year before could no longer buy what it could have bought then. The quality of savings had been impaired by 10 percent. Our confidence in our savings had been correspondingly damaged. Many of our population began to say: If the money we save will not be as good next year as it is now, we had better buy more of the things we want now, and save less.

Actually we have just tested the water with our toes. If we stop this inflation now, no permanent damage will have been done.

We have survived a crisis. Once more we move on confidently and industriously under conditions where every man may keep for himself the produce of his labor and the fruits of his ingenuity.

Before too long it becomes apparent that some sections of our society are prospering much more than others. The more able and the more industrious men are well off, while the less able and the lazy are poor. Some are living next to the line of poverty. Time shows us that the second class is growing faster than the first class.

Now this is a democratic society and our policy makers obtain their posts by election. Some keen politicians quickly perceive that the votes of the poor outnumber the votes of the well-to-do. The experience of the counterfeiters has not gone unnoticed. If counterfeiting could just be legalized by a certain few who run the government, money could be manufactured to distribute as alms to the poorer part of the society. If these politicians could get enough votes to put them in power, they would be in a position to pass a law permitting a certain increase in the money supply by the government.

Accordingly these politicians direct their campaigns toward the larger and poorer segment of our new colony. Their message is that the society is very rich, that the present government is favoring the well-to-do; as a whole the colony is well able to provide a decent standard of living for all. If they are elected there will be benefits to the poorer sections of society regardless of whether their poverty arises from ill health or simply because they are lazy.

When these politicians obtain office they find only two methods by which they can fulfill their promise. One is to tax the well-to-do, and thus *legally* take property from those to whom it belongs and give it to those to whom it does not belong, *or* print more money and deliver the excess supply, in benefits, to the poorer sections of the society.

Both of these alternatives produce exactly the same result, and amount to exactly the same crime. As the counterfeiters were bandits ravaging others illegally, these politicians are bandits ravaging members of the society legally.

Once these people have been firmly installed in office they begin to pay themselves handsome salaries and to peddle their influence. They make very sure that they deliver on their promises to the poor in order to count on those votes at the next election.

The process that has begun may not ruin the society for some time, but the inevitable end of the policy is a continual depreciation in the value of the money and an impairment of the money as a store of value. Those who have enough shoes but who wish to save to buy a pair of shoes tomorrow will find, when tomorrow comes, that the money they have saved will only buy one shoe or will buy a pair of shoes of half the quality of the shoes they could have bought. This produces a very strong feeling *against* saving.

Meanwhile these new politicians have invented interest and loans. The depreciation of the value of money has caused a reduction of effort and a reduction of total productivity. In order to "get the economy rolling again," their answer is to make loans to those who wish to build houses and expand their businesses. In order to loan additional money they have to resort to the printing press. This money, of course, does not have the backing of goods. For a time this causes great prosperity. With these loans people hire labor to build roads and houses. Labor is scarce and hourly rates go up; and so on down the line. In spite of the fact that prices are constantly rising, the printing press of these legal bandits turns out enough money so that the society is still moving ahead, and the man on the street says of the rising prices: "So what, I am better off than ever before. If this is the result of inflation, I'm in favor of it."

Simultaneously with the invention of the loans came the invention of interest on the loans to pay for the *risk*. The additional money needed to meet interest demands an even larger money supply. Interest mounts year after year and interest mounts on interest. (The U.S. Government had to provide over thirty billion dollars to pay this interest on its debt in 1975 alone.) It now becomes necessary to create even more money to keep up with the interest—or, on the other hand, to tax the well-to-do at a higher rate to pay for the mounting debt built on interest.

We have launched into an era of full-fledged inflation, and already, before the society realizes it, we are in a position where it will be extremely painful to halt. For one thing, all of the interest that has accumulated is in the form of money that is in *excess* of goods and services available. Loans on the banks are in excess of goods available in Freedonia. If lenders get scared and call these loans, business will go bankrupt and people will be out of work. But printing more money will keep the wolf from the door for a while.

Halting this inflation is going to throw the society into a recession, and consequently a political furor. Politicians who will spell out the truth will be denounced as cruel people, unsympathetic to the plight of the poor and deliberately promoting unemployment and poverty. These people will not be able to gain office.

It is becoming pretty obvious that the inflationists are in the saddle and that it will be impossible to unseat them; and that the process will go on—erratically perhaps—until they are destroyed by the collapse of the economy and starving peasants beating at their doors with clubs and pitchforks. If the process is allowed to go on long enough, it will end in revolution—indeed chaos.

That has happened in history many times, and the tipoff as to when this process is under way is when money begins to lose its store of value.

It is exactly here that most kings, dictators, and even democratic governments go astray. They are kept constantly aware of the mandatory function of money as a "medium of exchange," but they conveniently forget the equally important prerequisite, the "store of value."

That's because the deterioration of the "store of value" requirement does not show up at once, and, by the time it does show up, the temptations toward inflation have become so strong that it is easier to further reduce the store of value by a tiny percentage than it is to check the inflation.

The store of value depreciates so gradually at first that no noticeable complaint arises. The increase of the depreciation is insidious. The population, like the patient camel, doesn't mind the addition of just one more pound on its back, then two pounds, and eventually ten pounds. But as surely as the back of the camel will eventually break, so will the currency of that society eventually collapse.

In this process money has gradually deteriorated from representing real and existing wealth in its function as a medium of exchange into only an exchange *vehicle*—irredeemable in wealth, but circulated and accepted because of an overhanging confidence from its *past*. When finally it reaches a point where confidence fails and it is liable to be rejected in payment of a debt, the politicians are forced to pass a law that demands that people accept it at the face value imprinted upon it. They call it *legal tender*.

By Government edict it will bear the following inscription, which appears on the currency of the United States today, "This note is legal tender for all debts, public and private."

Notice how this was unnecessary in the early history of Freedonia. It follows, therefore, that when real money exists, coercion is unnecessary. Correspondingly, when real money loses value because of dilution through legal counterfeiting, coercion (legal tender) becomes necessary. When coercion is necessary, liberty is in retreat.

Notice that when natural laws were not suppressed liberty was in full bloom. Coercion was unthought of.

Remember we have already established that economic laws cannot be breached without penalty—irrevocable, inescapable. Someone pays the penalty.

The penalty for inflation is the *loss* of the "store of value." So the penalty has been paid by those who have saved, and by those who have lent to the government and to others.

The nature of money is such that when it is ravaged by inflation it correspond-

29

ingly loses its store of value, so that a continually accelerating inflation is necessary to maintain the same purchasing power—and that it is not possible to stop the inflation without a collapse of inflation (drastic deflation).

The inflation in the Western world today has accelerated to the point where this *collapse* is a foregone conclusion.

That means the collapse of the inflated dollar perched on a trembling pyramid of credit, which has been building for more than three decades.

That means we have come to the end of an era, or that we are closely approaching the end.

How this came about in our Western world—and the enormous social consequences—and some desirable steps for the preservation of capital and a reasonably safe existence in the face of unprecedented social convulsions—all of these are the subjects of this book.

5

HISTORY OF INFLATION

Inflation is an expression of the universal desire to have something for nothing, and of the power of politicians to fulfill that desire simply by printing money. It is also a manifestation of our natural inclination to rationalize—to convert the wish into belief.

Thus, inflationary tendencies are rooted in our nature, similar to greed, fear, and lust. Inflation is an aspect of nature in operation; it has been with us since money was invented as a medium of exchange. We can therefore expect to be plagued with inflation forever.

Stability—once re-established—will always be adulterated by a new army of wishful politicians. Once started, inflation always rises to a climax and the climax is always the same—collapse.

Money was used by the Egyptians at least 5,000 years ago; and with the help of hard money and the confidence resulting from hard money, Babylon became the center of world civilization and power. The city of Ur was a city of gold. It's interesting to observe that while Babylon attained grandeur via hard money, it reached even greater grandeur as it debased its money. But the debasement brought the end.

The king of Ur devised a scheme for wealth much greater than the wealth of his limited gold. As a custodian, he issued receipts—IOUs— and loaned out at interest the great wealth from the treasury of Ur. The stimulation of the doubling or the tripling of the wealth gave rise to visions of UTOPIA as it produced the world's greatest BOOM.

But as this immense purchasing power swelled, the claims on gold increased until they exceeded the gold. Foreign claims as a result of imports, plus domestic claims, exhausted the gold supplies of Ur. Still the IOUs circulated. After a long time the swollen volume of IOUs caused people to demand more of them. Inflation was in full swing.

Undaunted, the king of Ur, facing the fact that it took more money to buy the same goods, continued the expansion. He still had lots of silver. With the adroitness of a monetary expert, he extricated himself by a very neat device. He declared that the value of silver was equal to gold.

For some time Babylon advanced on a currency of silver equivalent to gold. But an uneasy feeling that this situation was not quite solid caused people to demand real silver faster than they had demanded real gold in the beginning. Soon there was no silver.

The next step was to declare that copper had a value equal to silver. This didn't work as long. It served rather as a confirmation of the decline in the value of money, and the collapse was at hand. Now, with its back against the wall, Babylon moved to its last retreat. It declared that lead had a value equal to copper.

Then Babylon fell.

So human nature was not so very different in the time of Babylon than in 1968 when the world's most affluent and most powerful nation declared that *paper* had a value equal to gold, and actually got other countries to agree to issue *paper gold* as a reserve asset of world money under the dignified name of Special Drawing Rights.

Babylon's gold and silver had fled to other lands. Assyria became the great center. Later Persia. Alexander the Great took Persia's gold, and Greece replaced Persia. All these countries developed through their energy, advanced thought, and productivity, and amassed great wealth. Silver and gold *measured* this wealth.

The same gold and silver later helped build the mighty empire of Rome, but there too the coin-clipping soon started. Debasement of money was under way. The debasement of Rome's currency led to the refusal of its legions to perform as soldiers, which led to the collapse of the Roman Empire.

Without exception, and throughout the trading history of mankind, the substitution of watered-down money for real money, and the continuing dilution, has marked the end of affluence and, later, influence.

Probably the three greatest *Declarers* in the history of civilization have been Babylon, Kublai Khan, and the U.S.A.

The Great Khan, ruling, with absolute authority, the largest kingdom ever known to man, stretching from Hungary to the China Sea, *declared* money at will and put his absolute power behind the declaration.

The writings of Marco Polo in the thirteenth century, as it turns out, described two monetary systems separated by 700 years. Marco Polo wrote:

"It is by this means that the Great Khan (U.S.A.) may have, and in fact, has more treasure than all the kings of the world. These pieces of paper are issued with as much solemnity and authority as if they were pure gold or silver, and on every piece a variety of officials whose duty it is, have to write their names and put their seal. And the Khan (U.S.A.) causes every year to be made such a vast quantity of this money, which costs nothing, that it must equal in amount all the treasures of the world.

"With these pieces of paper the Khan (U.S.A.) causes all payments on his (U.S.A.) account to be made, and he (U.S.A.) makes them pass current universally over all his kingdom (country) and possessions and territories, and whither-so-ever his power and sovereignty extends. And nobody however important he may think himself, dares to refuse them on pain of death."

It will be distressing for the money managers in Washington to read that the Great Khan (with all his power) could only make this last for 27 years. Paper money issues of 1260 depreciated by one-fifth by 1287. At that time the Great Khan recalled all monetary units and gave one new one for five old ones.

In another 80 years his empire had collapsed.

It is interesting to note that since 1944, about 30 years, the U.S. currency has deteriorated in purchasing power about five to one but that, so far, this exceeds the staying power of Kublai Khan's money by four years. The Great Khan had the advantage that he could put whole cities to the torch if they refused his money. U.S. propaganda, extolling the virtues of the paper dollar, has evidently been more effective than the sword and the fires of Kublai Khan. Nevertheless, if we are to be realistic, we must seriously doubt that the day of the big exchange can be far off.

Or so it seems. But hold on for a minute! It has been widely assumed that the solution devised by the Great Khan will be the inevitable solution to the inflation of the U.S. dollar—an exchange of several old ones for one new one. I myself was among the first to propose that this would happen, but I had not thought deeply enough.

When there is a massive overhang of credit, totally beyond any means of repayment—that credit must eventually be liquidated. There is no escape. The credit can be liquidated by one of two means. The first was that of the Great Khan—wipe it out by declaring the value of the debt to be only a fraction of what it was originally. A man had lent a hundred dollars. Now we say we will give 100 of the new dollars for 500 of the old dollars. But you who lent the money will get 100 of our currency, which, of course, is the new dollars. That is one way.

The second way that the massive debt can be liquidated is through bankruptcy. That is to say, default. A man lent a hundred dollars. The debtor goes broke and says to the man simply, "I'm sorry—I can't pay you back—I don't have any money."

The first answer means increased inflation. The second answer means deflation; that is, bankruptcy and depression. The great argument during 1975 was which route would be taken to liquidate the massive and plainly impossible structure of debt—deflation or inflation. The former—the route of the Great Khan—would be the easier. But there is one fundamental difference between the position of the U.S.A. and that of the Khan. He was the absolute ruler of all the lands where his currency circulated. The U.S. currency circulates throughout the world and is the basis for all world money; but the United States does not have the sovereign power to pass laws for the countries beyond its borders. This is a very complicated subject and will be discussed at greater length further on. To date, the military might of the United States has been used via implication and polite threat, conveyed, up to this point, by propaganda rather than guns.

It has been the military power of the United States that has given credence to its threat to withdraw its troops from Europe—laying countries defenseless before Communism—unless the dependent countries of Europe should continue to accept the engraved-paper promises. Germany had to buy billions of irredeemable dollars.

Kublai Khan's money rested finally solely on the signatures of his officials whose duty it was to affix their names. If you will examine the currency in your pocket you will find that it is the law of the land that "This note is legal tender for all debts, public and private," and you will see that certain officials have affixed their names—George P. Shultz, John A. Connally, Henry H. Fowler, David M. Kennedy—all of them monetary replicas of the officials of Kublai Khan.

It seemed that the fall of the Roman Empire taught mankind a lesson to remember: subsequent to that epoch inflations have nearly always resulted only from war. War necessitates an unbalanced budget—more politely known today as deficit spending.

War causes the ruler, or the government, to speed up production and to decrease relatively the amount of consumer goods. This puts everybody to work at higher wages without producing a corresponding amount of consumer goods and services. Unless the government coffers happen to be bulging with savings, it must create new money; and since there are no goods and services to match the new money, prices go up and inflation has commenced.

An example of this kind of inflation were the worthless assignats of France that blossomed and survived for seven years, from 1789 to 1796. Since this is not a history book we need not go into the details except to note that the result of the inflation once again was the collapse of the money.

The most dramatic modern example of the ruins left by the fires of inflation—once out of control—was the German inflation of the 1920s. To understand it you must understand a basic characteristic of inflation. *The decline of confidence in money accelerates faster than the decline in value of the money—once the confidence decline is in full swing.*

The decline of confidence is usually triggered first by the repeal of gold convertibility. This makes a few citizens suspect something is fishy. Inflation starts slowly here and builds as the feeling of insecurity grows.

Germany lost the war in 1918. In the following two years the government doubled the money supply. But prices had increased by five times; the public was discounting the value of money faster than the government was printing it; the erosion of confidence outpaced the erosion of value. The public feared the depreciation of its savings and, to protect them and to maintain some real value, it began to exchange its money for *things,* bidding prices up higher and higher.

By the end of 1920 prices had increased 14 times. But there they reached a plateau. They had reached a point where people thought they were ridiculous. The buying stopped; the money stabilized for about six months. But by about the middle of 1921, people became nervous again. Nothing had happened to confirm the stability of commodities at these levels. For no reason that one can nail down, a new spending spree started in the last half of 1921, and in this six-month period the value of money fell drastically as the printing presses raced to produce enough money to match the prices that were being bid higher and higher. It now took 37 marks to buy what one mark had bought at the time of the armistice. Money had lost two-thirds of its value in six months.

In the next six months, by January 1923, money went up 2,785 times. Now there was no hope. The inflationary fire was raging in full force. Money, as a store of value, was no longer even a concept. It was better to have a cow today at a high price than perhaps only a leg of lamb a month from now. In the next six months money went up 194,000 times. And in the following four months, by November 1923, it had gone up 726 billion times.

One mark at the time of the armistice would have bought as much as 726 billion in November 1923. Every German was a billionaire.

All bonds, all savings, had been wiped out.

During the time of the medium inflation a doctor borrowed from the bank and bought a dairy herd. Three months later he sold one cow and paid for the herd.

This isn't likely to happen again, but it serves as an object lesson in that it shows what public psychology can do to money that is not backed by anything *real.*

"Irrational!" cried the money managers of Germany.

"Irrational!" cried the treasury officials of the United States when the unredeemable dollars swamped the money markets of the world.

It is important to remember that if the money had any intrinsic value, or was redeemable for any amount of intrinsic value, this never could have happened. The only irrationality on the part of the public was that they fled from the money a little faster than they needed to.

At the height of the German inflationary storm money was losing value every hour. Factories paid their workers three times a day, and wives had to be Johnny-on-the-spot to collect the husband's money to get to the grocery store to buy some food before the prices again doubled the next day. But, alas, the shops were empty!

What farmer would sell his goods—his beef, his milk, his potatoes— for money that tomorrow would be worth half as much as it was today?

What worker would arise at seven in the morning to sweat for eight hours to receive money that would buy nothing tomorrow?

The economy was in complete collapse.

The monetary wizards of the United States have been propounding and repeating the old saw that the value of the dollar relies upon the productivity of the nation rather than upon any intrinsic worth. But the German case makes the fool of them. Germany enjoyed productivity, but the increasingly worthless paper mark destroyed that productivity and destroyed the economy.

If Kublai Khan was the model for the U.S. Treasury's method of monetary growth, Hitler was the prototype for its philosophy. It was Adolf Hitler who said, January 29, 1937:

"For the nation does not live from the fictitious value of money but rather from the actual production to which money itself gets value. This production is the real business of our currency and not a bank or treasury full of gold."

There is no doubt that gold itself does not make a nation rich. There is hardly any less doubt that it *measures* the wealth of a nation.

There is little doubt that, under the strictest restraint, money can function both as a medium of exchange and as a store of value, as we have seen in our sample colony in Chapter 3. Unfortunately there is also little doubt that, without the *discipline of a commodity*, managers and politicians will inevitably tamper with the money supply in pursuance of the human frailty to want something for nothing, and the human ability to rationalize a wish into a belief.

6

THE NATURE OF INFLATION

Just as the nature of money is a reflection of human nature, so the nature of inflation is a reflection of human nature. And the nature of human beings is a cosmic natural law.

It is an integral part of the nature of man that his desires are without limit; as opposed to all other species, whose desires fall within the limits of food, shelter, and reproduction. Since man's desires are limitless, his want of goods is limitless, and therefore his want of money is limitless.

He has come to learn that money means goods and the services of others. In his normal life it has never occurred to him that if the money he receives is in excess of the available goods, that money cannot, of course, represent goods. So the general public never realizes that inflation is taking place until it experiences inflation's consequences in the market place. The natural reaction to this is to demand higher wages. The higher wages, if granted, only increase the amount of money—*but not the amount of goods*—unless production increases correspondingly. So the addition of that inflationary purchasing media has done nothing for the worker.

And it is a natural fact that an artificial increase in purchasing media cannot be of the slightest benefit to the collective population. But successive increases in purchasing media, and resulting price increases, cause the population to begin to have less respect for the money. Thus we see the inception of a vicious circle that, once begun, can rarely be checked without a return to a total quantity of money *commensurate* to the total amount of goods and services. This always means a temporary contraction or recession, or, in extreme cases, depression.

Governments don't usually have the courage to accept the remedy. Instead they temporarily fool the worker by creating additional purchasing media and gradually set themselves up for an inevitable fall.

Since the time lag is considerable between the commencement of inflation and the final collapse, the politicians in power are not inclined to worry about the future. Their main aim is a pleasant present.

When John Maynard Keynes was reminded that someday we would have to pay off the enormous debt, his reply was, "Someday we will all be dead." He failed to mention that the upcoming generation wouldn't be dead, and the people who were now lending money wouldn't all be dead by the time its value had depreciated. It was typical of money managers and politicians, and typical of human nature, to defer the bad effects to the future.

Since it is human nature for those in power to resist the painful steps necessary to halt inflation, the tendency always is first to condone it, then assist it; until, finally out of hand, it prepares the ground for its own collapse.

History amply proves this thesis. A few politicians and bankers will make an effort to correct the situation, but, as soon as they see the face of the upcoming recession, they lose their nerve and go for the palliative of increasing the money supply, which temporarily once again satisfies the workers.

President Nixon, in 1969, vowed to control inflation and balance the budget. In six months he was confronted with a crashing stock market and the threat of bankruptcy throughout the nation. The vision of the upcoming disaster arising out of the long inflation would have been enough to deter even a mighty Caesar. Nixon and his banker, Arthur Burns, raced to push the button that would start the printing presses rolling again. From 1970 to 1974 we saw the greatest increase in the money supply of the world since money had been invented. The grim reaper confronting the United States was nothing short of chaos, and perhaps revolution. More money would at least delay Armageddon. By 1975 Arthur Burns was finding it difficult to push more money out. (We shall examine the reason for that later.)

So far we have seen, and we can conclude, since it is almost a natural law arising from human nature, that *inflation, once established, will always accelerate—when it is under the arbitrary control of human beings.*

Arbitrary control of the money supply can only take place under conditions of fiat money. It can never happen when money is exchangeable for a commodity, for the simple reason that the authorities—unlike Jesus—are unable to make a hundred fishes out of one or, indeed, even 101 fishes from 100.

Having understood that inflation is as certain as death and taxes when the money supply is under the control of mere men, we can now read the following from the *Encyclopaedia Britannica* with a degree of enlightenment:

> Until the 1930s, inflation had been generally regarded as an infrequent problem . . . no important inflation or deflation had in fact occurred for more than a hundred years before 1930, except as the consequence of war . . .
>
> One reason and probably the most powerful, for the infrequency of major inflation or deflation before the great depression of the 1930's was the widespread use of the gold standard. This system limited the issue of paper money and bank deposits to the level which the public, able to exchange money freely for gold, was willing to hold instead of gold.
>
> Free gold convertibility under the gold standard proper, or a fixed money-to-gold ratio set by legislation as an alternative, was completely effective (except when abrogated in wartime) *in setting limits to the power of government to acquiesce in inflation.*

It is no coincidence that during a century of stability the king of money in the world was the British pound; and Britain was on the gold standard and the pound was fully and freely convertible to gold. The hundred years up to 1914 saw the greatest progressive growth in the history of mankind. Generally speaking it was characterized by falling prices rather than by rising prices. A million dollars left as a bequest in 1820 was still worth a million dollars to the grandchildren at the dawn of the twentieth century—and more. But a million-dollar bequest of 1940 was worth no more than $300,000 by 1970; and no more than $200,000 by 1975. It's no coincidence that in the first case the world was to all intents and purposes on the gold standard, and in the second case the world was on the gold-exchange standard.

The enormous difference between these two systems and the deceptiveness of the second in its early stages will be discussed in the next chapter.

It should be clear by now to any reader that man, by his very nature, is not to be trusted as the custodian of the money supply, and that for the benefit of all mankind an immutable discipline must be imposed. The only immutable discipline is a commodity. In 5,000 years the most satisfactory commodities have been either gold or silver.

A primary argument against gold has always been that it is utterly stupid for men to fritter away their time in the bowels of the earth digging up gold and processing it, only to bury it again in vaults. Gold is superfluous to human needs and its production is a waste of time. You cannot eat gold.

You cannot eat a Fairbanks Morse scale, but there is no other way to keep your butcher honest. There could be no trade, and therefore no progress, without the use of millions of scales and rulers. These are safeguards to honesty, safeguards against avarice. Immutable measurements are mandatory to trade and therefore to progress.

The tiny percentage of world population engaged in extracting gold from the earth is surely less than the percentage engaged in the manufacture of scales and balances and measuring devices of every kind. It is a small price for society to pay in return for monetary stability.

As for storage, a million dollars at the $35 price occupies but one cubic foot. All of the gold in the world, and saved since the dawn of time, amounts to about 80 billion dollars and can be stored in a room 50 x 50 x 32 feet.

The Central Banks can put their present total of gold in a room 25 x 50 x 32 feet. Big deal!

WHAT THIS MEANS TO YOU

It means that gold is the manifestation of the essence of the accumulation of the liquid wealth of mankind. It means that since the central bankers have half of it, and refuse to part with one ounce of it, the central bankers themselves consider it to be a last resort for monetary defense. It means that gold is the most valuable and reliable money in the world.

If gold means all that to the central bankers, it should mean to you that at least part of your assets could be concentrated in this indestructible wealth, especially in view of the tumultuous events that we face in the seventies, as you will see in the balance of this book. It means rather than keeping your money in cash in bank accounts, or in safe-deposit boxes, or in the form of bonds, at least a portion of this wealth should be invested in gold coins. Since January 1, 1975, you have also been able to buy gold bars, which you can store in strongboxes or in a good deep hole in your own backyard.

Low premium gold coins, however, such as the Krugerrand and the Mexican peso are among the best to accumulate. The gold coin of Panama is legal tender there, which makes it interesting. As this is written months before publication, it is hard to say which will be the best gold coins to buy. You should make those inquiries of a reputable coin dealer.

7

THE GOLD STANDARD

Let us return to our colony, and let us, this time, imagine 10 million dollars of gold at $35 per ounce, representing all of our goods according to our price lists. Let us imagine that we had set up a council to administer our money, and agreed that we would print paper certificates equivalent to the amount of gold and redeemable in coins of gold to whoever might demand them.

As soon as our people found they could always get the coins in return for the paper, and knew without question that the coins were there, they would prefer the paper because of its convenience. Even if, at times, they became distrustful and demanded coins in place of the paper, ready fulfillment of demand would instantly demolish any misgivings. Reassured, citizens would, as a matter of convenience, quickly drift back to the paper.

As our society produced and progressed and built more houses and grew more crops, we would find ourselves with goods in excess of money. In that case one of three things would have to happen.

(a) The price of commodities would gradually go down—nothing wrong with that. Money that had been saved would buy more.

(b) We would have to increase the value of the gold. If we had 25-percent increase in goods we would have to increase the value of the gold 25 percent, and have a 25-percent increase in the money supply. If we had doubled our store of value collectively, we would have to double the money supply and therefore double the price of gold.

(This gives the lie to those who say that there is not enough gold in the world to back increased commerce and increased productivity. Nonsense. It's only a matter of arithmetic. It's a question of assigning a monetary value to gold commensurate with the goods and services available to the society. There is absolutely no such thing as insufficient gold to make a gold standard work—except in the case where all of the people might be demanding the coins. In that event the coins might be too small to handle, requiring admixture with an alloy for practical use.)

(c) If we didn't want prices to fall, and if we didn't devalue the money, we would simply have to increase the supply of gold by finding some.

Surely this ought to be clear to our economists. Unfortunately it isn't. But history demonstrates that it's true.

Consider the following from *Chambers' Encyclopaedia:*

> In epochs when the national economy was dependent upon supplies of a money metal, inflation was only possible if relatively exceptional quantities of the metal became available—as in Europe, and particularly Spain, between 1550 and 1650, on the arrival of the produce of the silver mines of Spanish America.

This was an unusual event in history and the increased availability of silver couldn't last. As soon as the increase stopped, the resulting mild inflation was also throttled. Runaway inflation was an impossibility.

The encyclopaedia continues:

> The possibilities of considerable inflation of this kind diminished, so that the gold discoveries of the second half of the 19th century, although of unprecedented size, had only small and gradual effect on price levels.

The truth is that production of precious metals can't take place fast enough to cause serious inflationary problems, whereas the production of fiat currency, produced by the whim of man, can proceed at any speed desired.

The encyclopaedia continues:

> Where, however, currencies take the form of inconvertible paper, and can thus be expanded at will, no natural limit exists to their inflationary possibilities . . . The need for additional currency commonly arises from the exigencies of an unbalanced budget, and since such exigencies occur most acutely in time of war (when also, supply of consumers' goods tends to fall) severe inflations are usually found to arise out of war-time conditions.

If our colony were to find that a hitherto-unexpected native population intended to attack the colony—perhaps destroy it—it would be necessary, in the interest of the safety of all, to prepare for war. Workers would have to drop many of their constructive projects, even to the extent of leaving the fields, to make spears and swords and, if possible, guns and bullets. The production of these laborers would add nothing to the general goods and services available and desired in the normal life of the colony.

These laborers would nevertheless have to be paid, even though the fruits of their labors could not be sold. It would be necessary either to borrow the savings from our people or to issue more money against the gold (inflation) to keep this war effort going. If the war lasted a long time, extra taxes would have to be imposed and the savings increasingly consumed. The injection into the purchasing media of more than the equivalent of the total usable goods and services could not help but make all the money worth less, and thus reduce the value of all savings of the society. That would be the price our colony would have to pay to defend itself.

The net result would be a reduced standard of living during the war and even thereafter, to make up for destruction and wasted effort.

But as long as we remain on the gold standard, with our paper redeemable in the metal, albeit in smaller quantity, confidence in the money could not be stampeded and the inflation could not go unnoticed. When the war was over, our monetary situation would return to normal. All prices would be higher, as a result of lost production and of destruction during the war.

However, it would be possible that during the war itself we might not experience much inflation, despite the increased money supply. Production of goods would have declined to the point where wartime rationing was necessary. The wages of our workers and our warriors, over and above the goods available, would go into savings. When the war was over the people would want to spend their money, and they would bid up the prices of available goods in the market place, and that is where we would notice the inflation resulting from war.

Still, in all, in the case of a gold-backed currency, the entire population would be aware of the true devaluation of the currency as a result of war. As long as the government did not increase the money supply beyond the new rate necessitated by the war; as long as it would publicly announce the value of the dollar compared with the gold reserve, no ruinous inflation could result, simply because no more money could be created.

Gold would have performed an incalculable service by its validation of the measurement of the price we have paid for defense.

Our colony would find that since one of its dollars would (as a result of the war inflation) buy fewer goods at home than it bought before the war, it would also buy fewer goods in the countries with which we might be trading. The value of the dollar would be established domestically. Whatever that value turned out to be, it would be solid; and other countries would trust it.

However, if after the war we industriously rebuilt our nation, we would find that our efforts were gradually increasing the volume of goods once again until they equaled what they had equaled before. As the goods increased in our colony, and as we did not, under the gold standard, print bogus money, we would find the price of things actually coming down, as the total volume of goods rose in relation to the total volume of money. By our industry we should recover to the point where our money had the same value in goods as it had before the war.

In all of this time we should have known exactly where we stood through an immutable and precise measurement of our wealth, as precise and impartial as the Fairbanks Morse scale—the commodity gold.

And there, in a nutshell, you have the reason why the political leaders of a country that is going downhill despise gold—*its ability to measure and to clearly announce the results of their management.* In a country that is making real progress, politicians usually come to love gold, as they did in the United States until the early 1960s.

There was never a greater gold-hater in the world than Adolf Hitler. The value of German money was enforced by law. He was still able to produce a miracle. The value of the German mark was, for a period, even solid outside the country. Antigold people will point to this sometimes as an example of the superfluous nature of gold. They haven't seen the whole picture.

When a large part of the productive capacity of our colony is diverted toward unproductive ends, and when we have to create money to pay these unproductive workers, it is a natural law that there are fewer commodities available for the population per unit of money. You have inflation whether you like it or not, and either one of two things must happen:

(a) the price must go up;

(b) the purchase of commodities must go down.

Authoritarian states choose the second because it masks the adulteration of the money. Goods are strictly rationed. Unable to buy goods, the workers turn the money into savings. The excess money becomes *backed-up* in bank accounts—unspendable. Prices can stand still if there is no increase in the volume of goods purchased.

At this point they do not recognize that the "saved" money is without substance because there are no goods in the marketplace to represent it. The inflation has been there all the time, but it does not emerge until the savings are released into the marketplace in competitive bidding for limited goods. Only then do they find that the "saved" money that gave such comfort in their bank books was really an *illusion*.

Fiat money has fooled the population.

8

GOLD CAN CAUSE INFLATION

For a hundred years following the wars the economy in the land of Freedonia was strong and stable. The mines of the country produced just about enough gold to keep up with the increasing productivity of the land. As long as this balance was maintained they had neither inflation nor deflation. For more than a hundred years a dollar was always worth a dollar.

If a boy earned a dollar chopping wood when he was ten years old, and if he had put that away in a piggy bank and forgotten about it, he could recover it when he was 70 years old and buy the same necktie that he would have bought for a dollar when he was a boy. Had he put the money at interest he would have earned something each year, because money was lent in the land of Freedonia for sound business enterprises.

Money could always be lent for goods on their way to market. For instance the farmer, with wheat in his granary, could borrow on that wheat, because it was known to have real value, and it would sooner or later reach the warehouse. It was considered to be goods on the way to market.

It was possible even to borrow money to buy seed grain if the farmer already had his farm and his horses and his plow and a reputation to back him up. The seed grain would probably become grain and could be considered goods on the way to market.

In the decades to follow, however, this concept of banking would be wiped out. They would stretch it to include an advance to buy the machinery to plow the land to seed the grain, to harvest the grain, to bring it to market. Then later on, in the days of heavy speculation and easy credit, this would be extended to buy the land on which to plant the grain with the machinery purchased on credit to be eventually harvested and brought to market.

But in the days when Freedonia was strong and the banking system was stable, loans were always repaid. The money supply always represented the goods and services in existence as they increased or decreased. No one got rich through speculative land deals, nor through the clever manipulation of other people's money. But shoe factories sprang up along with mills and mines, and a growing fraternity of merchants to distribute these products to the population.

This is not to say that the Freedonians were satisfied. They always wanted more, and wanted it quicker. They always needed and wanted more money than they had. There was always a complaint about the scarcity of money. Imagine the rejoicing then when, one day, the news came that gold had been discovered in the far eastern corner of the country. So rich was this discovery that nuggets could be lifted from the surface. The excitement was electric.

With all this new money, thought the Freedonians, everyone would be rich. Everyone could buy all he needed. And so the mines began to hum; and the gold began to pour into the vaults of the Freedonian treasury as it issued currency for the gold.

Alas, the dream was short-lived.

All that happened was that when the gold supply was doubled the money supply had also been doubled, but the amount of goods and services available had not increased a bit. In a very short time it became clear that it now took two Freedonian dollars to buy what one Freedonian dollar had bought before the gold discovery. Those who had cashed in early on the gold had benefited, of course, but generally, and in the country as a whole, the consequences of the gold discovery produced more harm than good. While the early birds had benefited, it had been at the expense of others.

This great discovery of gold had really amounted to the same thing as if the Freedonian government had suddenly decided to double the money supply without any backing.

That has happened at least twice in our recorded history. Alexander the Great was the first to suffer from an excessive accumulation of gold. He raided the vaults of every country he conquered and sent the gold home to Greece. Money was issued to match this very fast accumulation of wealth. The result was inflation, and a bad one.

It happened to the Spaniards after they discovered the great gold hoards in the new world.

All this is to show that there is nothing magic about gold and, therefore, nothing magic about the Gold Standard.

The *reason* that gold has served monetary stability so well is that it is so scarce, and that its production is quite stable and quite slow. It acts as a great balance wheel. No other metal or commodity can fill this bill. Only once in history has a bonanza discovery of gold resulted in inflation. The discovery of gold in South Africa had a similar, but lesser, effect.

Today the discovery of gold in the amounts found by the Spaniards in the new world would have very little effect on the world, because *percentagewise* it would be such a small part of the money supply. In those days, percentagewise, it was a very impressive factor.

It is very important to recognize that those who back the gold standard are not simply nuts who have a sort of *religion* relating to gold. Gold could as well be nothing more than black coal, or iron, as far as the gold standard adherents are concerned. They believe in it only because a lot of it cannot easily be found, and therefore it acts as the stabilizer par excellence.

9

THE GOLD-EXCHANGE STANDARD

To this point we have been speaking in generalizations, but only with a view to linking these generalizations to the conditions existing in the United States today and throughout the world. The premise is that if we can accurately assess and clearly evaluate the reality of the current conditions we may be able to get a reading on the direction in which we are moving and to see whether we are running into an obstacle, or over a cliff.

If we were to find that this inflation will continue until it collapses, that would be very valuable information on which to base our investments, and indeed to plan our lives—because in this modern society the population has been promised so much, and has been led to expect so much, that the collapse of inflation and the resulting depression, would most certainly touch off violent resentment from the masses.

The foreclosure of mortgages and the closing of banks, the destruction of savings, and riots on a scale never before imagined could, under the right conditions of mass psychology and mob violence, result in conditions similar to those of the French Revolution.

Probably the first reaction of the government to pacify the raging public will be to print enough money to keep the banks in business and stimulate employment to where workers could pay their rent and feed themselves—even though this new influx of inflation could only worsen and intensify the dying convulsion of the present era, the age of inflation.

That term owes its name to the most astute economist of this century, Jacques Rueff. Rueff traced inflation's roots to the gold-exchange standard and philosophized more than ten years ago that unless the system were corrected it would destroy our Western civilization.

The gold-exchange standard is a 50-year-old invention. It grew out of the inflation following World War I, when it was discovered that there was not nearly enough gold to back the large new quantities of money in circulation. Rather than face the fact that money had lost purchasing power, the authorities thought to remedy the situation by conserving gold.

So the gold-exchange standard was, from the moment of its birth, a gimmick. There was a deficiency in the quality of money. The gold-exchange standard was invented to *cover it up*.

Had a fundamentalist been in charge of the Genoa Convention of 1923, the inflation tree would never have been planted. For it was in its beginning an outright defiance of natural law.

The Genoa Convention proclaimed that you can dispose of your cake to others without losing any yourself.

If I lend you $2,000, that is $2,000 for you to use; but, at the same time, it must mean that I am not now able to use that $2,000 for myself.

The Genoa Convention defied that proposition.

The United States dollar and the British pound had come to be accepted as the equivalent of gold. The Genoa Convention said that since these currencies are as good as gold and are interchangeable with gold, they may be held in the reserves of Central Banks and be considered in every respect the equivalent of gold.

There is hardly any doubt that the fathers of this convention were blind to the Frankensteinian nature of the infant they then released upon the world. Not for a moment did they dream that 50 years later their naive creation would smite them with such unremitting fury that the very foundations of civilization would rattle.

To understand this fully it is convenient to return to our highly prosperous country of Freedonia. Let's say Freedonia has a hundred million ounces of gold valued at $35 per ounce. Its total money supply then is $3,500 million in its checking accounts and currency.

Up to this time, if Freedonia had spent $100 million in a foreign land, its currency was of necessity reduced by exactly $100 million. It happened this way:

The foreign land, having received the Freedonia dollars from tourists or what not, presented them to the Freedonian Treasury for gold.

The Freedonia Treasury turned over $100 million of gold to that country. This meant that since Freedonia was on the gold standard it could not possibly have that $100 million for itself anymore. Its gold supply, and therefore its total money supply, had been reduced by exactly that amount. It now had $3,400 million.

Perhaps Freedonia was well able to afford this loan—or this expense —or this war—as the case might have been. The point is that while it was being used in the other country, *it was taken out of use in Freedonia.* The money supply in total among all the countries remained still the same.

But under the gold-exchange standard invented in Genoa that old-fashioned principle no longer applied.

Freedonia could spend the $100 million in Slobdovia, and Slobdovia would immediately take this money into its central bank reserves, and it would spend this money among other countries for perfume or guns or whatever, and other countries would accept it because it was as good as gold. Freedonia itself would not give up any gold. Its money supply, instead of being reduced, as had previously been the case, now remained the same.

So this $100 million, while it went abroad to be used for spending, at the same time stayed at home to be used for spending.

This was the gold-exchange standard. How could it help but double the money supply? But we must remember that at the same time there had not been the slightest increase in the total amount of goods and services available for the total money supply among the collective countries.

The effect was electric. Credit was greatly increased on the other side of the Atlantic, without cutting down on the credit on this side. The more British pounds and U. S. dollars that were lent and spent, the greater became the credit. Much of the money returned and was spent in Great Britain and the United States, increasing still further the money supply in these two countries—making money very plentiful.

Where, at one time, it was difficult to build a house with only 50 percent cash, and 50 percent borrowed, now a man might build with only 40 percent or perhaps 30 percent. At any rate, the more money that was issued the greater was the credit available; the bigger were the loans men could receive with which to build houses, start businesses, buy luxuries, and so forth.

Why wouldn't there be a boom?

As the available money was multiplied in the banking system (this usually amounts to about six times), large funds were available for investments of every kind, including the stock markets all around the world. The bidding went higher, then higher, then higher.

Once people began to see how easy it was to make money, more of it was placed in the stock market. There was general euphoria. Stock prices became related less to value than to a guess as to how much the next guy would pay to get the stock to sell later at a still higher price to someone else.

No one suspected we were building up to 1929. Prosperity was, in fact, so well assured that there was no longer need to pay the full price for stocks. Obviously they weren't going to go down. So it came to be that you could buy a stock for a hundred dollars, and borrow at least $50 on it from the bank. You paid the bank interest. Later the stock doubled. Everyone was happy.

Natural law had been abridged.

When this success was a proven fact, the margins were still further reduced until at last you could buy a hundred-dollar stock by only putting up $10 of your own money.

It is not the purpose here to go into the stock market crash of 1929 and the depression of the 30s. These were in fact sharp reminders that natural law had not been violated—nature had been mocked. All of the froth that had grown up around this extravagant idea of the gold-exchange standard was simply scooped off again—and with a heavy penalty. The bankruptcy of a huge Austrian bank sent out tidal waves like the eruption of a volcano in a small lake. There was the fall of the empire of Kreuger, the match king. One fall brought on another. Millionaires on Wall Street were knocked over like so many match sticks. Enormous paper fortunes went up in smoke.

As it turned out, those who thought themselves so rich had only been rich in thought. They had been rich in figures that were written in ink on some paper.

It had all been a grand illusion.

The insight into the nature of the gold-exchange standard must from the beginning be credited to Jacques Rueff. This French economist saw it instantly for what it was. But he had to be wrong. Weren't the events of the 20s proving what a great success the gold-exchange standard was?

Jacques Rueff was to see the event occur again, but not until much later, because in 1934 President Roosevelt went back to the gold standard. By devaluing the U. S. dollar he made it fully convertible internationally into gold. In order to do this he had to deprive U. S. nationals of their right to own gold—a right of which they were wrongfully deprived until January 1975. By this time gold had reached $200 an ounce, and their opportunity for gain had been lost.

Many, or even most, of the economists writing on the subject of 1929 and the depression of the 30s, have been so obtuse as to blame it on the gold standard. If these men had spent all of their lives learning how to be wrong, they couldn't have made a better success of it. There is not the *slightest* element of truth contained in the dissertations of those who say that depressions were caused by the gold standard. It's a matter of historical record that this sturdy sentinel had been traded off for the flashy new charms of the gold-exchange standard. The economists had been seduced!

In his book *The Crisis of World Inflation* William Rees-Mogg, editor of the *Times* of London, states, "Prices in Britain were very stable for the two hundred and fifty years after the Restoration with the exception of the Napoleonic period. *It is quite plausible that prices were about ten percent lower in 1913 than in 1661.*"

Any depressions or booms during the quarter-millennium of the gold standard had been minor waves on a stable monetary sea. Deflations and inflations were never more than ripples. They never could be more, because the discipline of gold snuffed out every unreality almost as soon as it arose. You could not fool yourself into thinking you were rich when before your very eyes you could see the gold pile shrinking.

10

THE BUST OF THE BOOM

No one could have told the speculators of 1928 and 1929 that the stock market would lose 90 percent of its value. They listened to the same slogans then as fell on the ears of the speculators of 1974, "Merrill Lynch is *BULLISH ON AMERICA*."

As the stock market got top-heavy, ever larger volumes of buying were required. Once it moved into reverse, enormous amounts of capital were required. It became fashionable to be "BULLISH ON AMERICA" —as if the degree of a man's patriotism could be measured by the extent to which he was willing to place his funds on the line. If you didn't want to bet on the stock market going up, you were next thing to a cop-out. You were not bullish on America. It wasn't exactly treason, but it took a pretty low type of character to be bearish on America.

That was the implication, and it demonstrates the irrationality of the investment community. It is an irrationality unfortunately that spreads to the monetary community, and even to the monetary managers.

In fifty years that much hasn't changed.

When the crash came it dealt with the inflationary abominations swiftly and effectively. When a stock selling at a hundred dollars goes to $10, 90 percent of the money supply in that share has simply been wiped off the face of the earth. And so billions upon billions were stripped from the money supply. The billions of inflationary hot air that had been pumped into the balloon were suddenly let out.

It was a good thing, because had it gone on the end of the binge could have only been worse.

It was an example to the world of what would happen if ever again it should apply this Alice-in-Wonderland philosophy—the gold-exchange standard.

When the citizens of Freedonia (U.S.A.) offered their gold certificates that guaranteed one ounce in gold, or ten ounces in gold, written above the great seal of Freedonia, the gold window was slammed down on their fingernails. All of the solemn promises were repudiated. The seal of Freedonia was revealed to be a farce.

This truth was not publicized, nor was it barely allowed to be thought. The official repudiation had to be cloaked in the terms of "the common good." So bankrupt was Freedonia and the world that repudiation had to be followed by confiscation.

Roosevelt ordered not only the cancellation of all gold contracts, but also that every citizen of the United States turn in his gold to the United States Treasury. He stripped the population of gold.

Now it was time for the edict that the currency notes were legal tender, and it was written upon them that they could be redeemed in "lawful money" of the United States. It was never defined what "lawful money" was. Later on, in the 1960s, this meaningless redemption clause was removed from all the notes so that all they amounted to was a piece of paper that assured the holder that it was indeed legal tender, and if the holder owed a debt to anybody, the creditor would be required to accept the note at face value in payment of the debt—no matter how much the purchasing power of the note had depreciated.

Freedonia as the "Originals" had known it was only a memory.

To thinkers of the present day the question must arise, however: who was responsible, Roosevelt, or his predecessors, the men at Genoa? Both must bear a share of the guilt.

Roosevelt had no choice but to devalue the dollar because it simply no longer represented the former standard weight in gold. There was just too much currency out against the existing gold. But instead of repudiation he might well have considered a devaluation of a larger scale so that the money supply and the gold supply would again be brought back into equilibrium, and internal convertibility preserved. The grand seal and the honor would have been retained to the highest degree possible.

People who go into bankruptcy and who simply do not have the assets to cover their debts, but who pay every last cent they can, are not in disgrace. But those who repudiate are never more to be trusted.

Roosevelt devalued the dollar from $20.67 for an ounce of gold to the point where it took $35.00 to buy an ounce of gold; and prohibited the trading of gold internally in the United States. External balances among countries still had to be settled by gold. There was no other way to settle them, because the gold-exchange standard had collapsed. There was nothing left but the gold standard. It was not a choice for Roosevelt. It was a last retreat. So, during the depression, the gold standard was in force. But it inherited the depression. It did not cause it.

Nevertheless the gold standard, being in force, got the blame for the depression. It was as if a country, after fighting for some years, was about to lose a war, was about to be destroyed—and then brought in some general who barely prevented it from being destroyed but who could not produce a victory. So the country would blame this last general for the disastrous war. There was no way the gold standard could miraculously pull the world out of the morass into which it had been thrust by the gold-exchange standard.

The milk had been spilt. The gold standard could not sponge it up again. There never had been that much money in the first place. The prosperity always had been a pseudo-prosperity. Under natural law there was no way the world could come out rich from the destruction and wasted effort of war; rich and better off than when it entered the war. Thus, instead of paying the price during the 1920s, the world paid the price during the 1930s.

The gold-exchange standard had simply delayed and, in doing so, intensified the penalty of war.

Economists will write for 50 years opposing theories of the intricate causes of the great depression, completely failing to understand that it was nothing more than the manifestation of a natural law: which means that if a stone is released it will drop; if a hand intervenes to delay the drop, it will still drop as soon as the hand is removed. The gold-exchange standard was the hand.

The depression was the price of the war and the additional penalty for trying to cover it up.

There is always a penalty for deceit—even with yourself. Anytime you fool yourself you will pay a penalty.

The enemies of the gold standard will point back to the depression, emphasizing that it still wasn't over in 1939 at the beginning of World War II; that we had, in fact, slipped again into depression in 1937. Had it not been for the war, they say, the gold standard might have kept us in depression forever.

No one knows when the depression would have ended. It is probable that even the years of depression had not yet paid for the massive devastation of World War I, including the almost incalculable amount of labor that was totally lost to consumer goods.

What we do know is that World War II unleashed another tidal wave of credit, far greater than the first. And that up to 1975 nobody has paid this bill either.

WHAT THIS MEANS TO YOU

It means that this entire bill is still to be paid. It means, therefore, that the savings that have gone into the destruction and that were thereby consumed now amount to little more than numbers on sheets of paper; they are largely fictitious. Most of the remaining wealth, when this is over, will be represented by properties that are real.

It means, therefore, from a practical standpoint, that you should transfer your assets, or at least a substantial portion of them, into the things that you need to sustain your existence and your comfort. The transformation of assets into a home that is fully paid must stand near the top of the list of wise investments at any time. And, in these times, as a retreat as well.

Beyond that, in times of great monetary uncertainty, holdings of gold and silver, probably in the form of coins, are the best remedy for the preservation of wealth.

11

ERA OF INFLATION IS BORN

The inflation of the 20s was too short-lived to classify as an era. It was rather an interlude. It amounted to a ten-year cancellation of the gold standard. The victorious powers tried the inflationary remedy. It ended in a bust. So they had to reverse themselves in 1934 and go back to the gold standard in America. The pound had been discredited and practically destroyed. The United States' dollar emerged as the world's most desired currency—a money still as good as gold internationally, albeit at a reduced price.

War presented the financiers with little problem. Even in our ideal colony of Freedonia in its early stages—operating on the gold standard —the mustering of resources for war was relatively easy. That is because in time of war people will willingly support their country with their savings. They will accept depreciation of their money. There is always this argument: If we lose the war, what good will our money do us? It is after the war that the money problem arises. It is after the war that the price of the destructive expenditures must be reckoned.

Many people, therefore, expected a depression after World War II. They simply could not see how we could lose so much time, waste so much effort, destroy so much—without paying the bill. We hadn't been that well off before the war. Surely it wasn't natural that all this waste could take place and we would find ourselves better off than ever, richer than ever before. If one were to believe that, he had to accept a new axiom: *"destruction brings wealth."*

People couldn't believe that, and they expected a depression.

By the fall of 1975 we hadn't had that depression yet. In 30 years we have had nothing but booms as a result of the war. Apparently the war has produced an enormous prosperity; and if we want to be prosperous we must keep on destroying.

We destroyed and wasted hundreds of billions of dollars collectively, and now are we better off than before?

Doesn't make sense. But here is the living proof—30 years of world prosperity. How come?

You and I know that the bill owed doesn't go away. You and I know that a quart of milk spilt is a quart of milk less. A farmer knows that if one of his fields is burned up, he has lost that much grain—no matter how much money the bank is willing to lend him, or for how long a period—even 30 years.

How did this 30-year miracle occur? The answer is simple:

The gold-exchange standard! The Bretton Woods Agreement.

In 1944 the powers met at Bretton Woods and constructed a new monetary system for the world. Well, not exactly. The self-same system they had put forth in Genoa in 1923 was to be fractured for a second time in 1968 when all the powers combined could not withstand the surging world demand for gold at $35 per ounce. In March of 1968 Bretton Woods was smashed. World gold sales were stopped. The fracture was papered over with the "two-tier gold system" under the now-infamous Washington Agreement.

On March 12, 1973, the Bretton Woods agreement, five years dead, was officially buried. As of that date there was no monetary system in the world. For on that date the Common Market countries decided to break any formal relationships of fixed parities with the American dollar.

Bretton Woods was built on two fundamental planks. One was the international convertibility of the dollar into gold at $35 per ounce. The other was a system of fixed parities by all countries as measured against the dollar, as measured against gold.

Nixon had closed the gold window and had so broken condition number one when, in August 1972, he refused to pay out gold for dollars at any price. The six countries of the Common Market broke the last vestige of fixed relationship on March 12, 1973, when they decided to float jointly as a unit. This meant they would measure their currencies one against the other internally—and the dollar could do what it liked. It would, in fact, be measured against them.

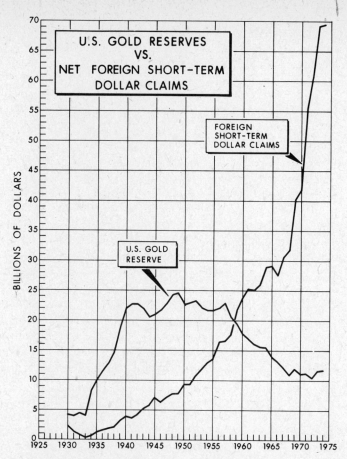

This graph shows the solid solvency of the United States Treasury in 1950—holding $25 billion in gold with only about $6 billion of outstanding claims. If all the creditors at once had converged on the U.S. gold pile they would have been paid off and the U.S. still would have had $19 billion in solid gold.

By 1960 the gold pile had declined to equal the outstanding claims and the United States—technically speaking—moving into insolvency. Kennedy recognized the dangerous trend and made dollar stability part of his election platform.

The Johnson administration could be aptly termed the era of stimulation: U.S. Treasury and administration officials closed their eyes to the danger of the expanding debt.

In 1968, following the Washington agreement, Central Banks agreed not to buy or sell gold and were pressured to promise not to ask for gold. As a consequence the U.S. gold stock remained stable thereafter. But the debts mounted to $60 billion by the end of 1971, and by the end of 1973 had reached an estimated total of between $80 and $100 billion, which was eight to ten times the existing gold stock. The price of gold would have to be multiplied eight to ten times for the United States to become barely solvent again—in other words to recover to the position where it stood in 1960. The frightening prospect of an 800 percent devaluation caused the United States to continue to resist gold convertibility, and to push the acceptance of imaginary money such as U.S. printing-press dollars and Special Drawing Rights.

But what could they all, or any of them, be measured against? Not a mark, not a franc, not a lira. There was only one thing in the world left for them to be measured against, and that was gold. In 5,000 years fundamentals had not changed.

But the public? After the most devastating war in history they had been rewarded with the greatest prosperity in history. Now all of a sudden—and apparently for no reason—prosperity was in question. What was wrong with the miracle known as the gold-exchange standard?

What was wrong with it, was that it was, from the first, a trick. There was nothing wrong when Jesus made many fishes out of two fishes. If—as we are told—the story is true, many fishes actually appeared and filled the bellies of the people. But when the magician makes many rabbits out of one rabbit, it is merely sleight of hand. It is a *deception*. And that is what was wrong with the gold-exchange standard.

At Bretton Woods the powers all agreed that the U.S. dollar—backed by nearly 25 billion in gold in the U.S. Treasury—was certainly as good as gold. Any and every foreseeable demand could be amply met, and more. Who would look forward to a day when the United States would spend so much more than it earned that it would accumulate debts with these other nations equivalent to its entire gold pile? More fantastic still, who would look forward to the day when it would incur debts even $10 billion in excess of its gold pile—yes, $20 billion—yes, $50 billion—yes, and by 1973, $80 billion, and by 1975 more than $100 billion. By its printing presses it would produce an amount of international debt certificates equivalent to three times the entire gold pile of 1945. What is more, it would have received goods and services for this created money. What is more, it had no way to pay for those goods and services already received.

But in 1945 who could look forward to such a day?

And so the gold-exchange standard, already described, and which in ten short years led to the most terrible depression in history, in 1944 had simply been hauled out of storage, refurbished, painted up, and put back into action under a new name—Bretton Woods.

The United States could spend hundreds of millions for the reconstruction of Europe, and the dollars would not come back to the Treasury to be redeemed for gold. So while the United States was spending this money abroad, it was at the same time spending it at home. Its money supply was not reduced by the amount of money it gave away or spent.

For $10,000 it could build a $10,000 house in Duluth, and at the same time a $10,000 house in Dresden.

The dollars were trusted in Dresden. The thing that people didn't see was that *someday*, somebody, somewhere, might become nervous about those dollars and—when he tried to use them to buy an equivalent amount of goods from someone else—he might meet reluctance to accept them at face value. At that time he would send them back to the United States and ask to be paid off in gold.

What people did not foresee was that when the United States refused to pay gold as it had pledged, the gold-exchange standard would be dead. The IOUs would not be collectible. The last guy with the money was like the guy at the end of the chain letter.

It was in fact a monstrous universal chain letter.

How such a thing could come about and go on was illustrated in one of the *Myers' Finance & Energy* newsletters in the section called the "Quiet Corner," July 18, 1969, here partially reproduced:

I have said that U.S. money is debt money. Some are puzzled by this: find it hard to fathom. Will you join me with your imagination for a moment?

Suppose that I am Howard Hughes. You are my creditor and I give you an IOU for one hundred dollars. (A check on the bank is an IOU of course). You give this to your service station mechanic. He accepts it readily. Howard Hughes can issue untold thousands of one hundred dollar IOU's, instantly acceptable anywhere.

Let us now suppose that Mr. Hughes does issue a million, even two million IOU's of a hundred dollars. People don't even bother to take them to the bank; they are just as good as money; just the same as money. With the confidence in this great empire, imagine these IOU's circulating freely. But these bills are large denominations; and wherever he can Mr. Hughes gets his men to pick them up and reissue ten dollar notes on green paper with his signature. Thus let's say we have one hundred million dollars in Hughes' currency. Is it money? That depends.

If Mr. Hughes is indeed a solvent as we thought, it is money. But whether it is money or not, it amounts to one hundred million dollars of Hughes' *debts*. Does it not?

Now suppose that Mr. Hughes has in the meanwhile engaged in ruinous ventures in airlines in China, movies in Italy, etc. Suppose he has lost and mortgaged his various plants and properties. Now is this Hughes' currency money?

No it is not. It represents Mr. Hughes' debts. It is debt money. It is MONETIZED DEBT.

The U.S. currency in your bank accounts today is exactly that: the monetized debt of the United States. The notes are convertible to nothing by the government itself; not wheat, not iron, not even straw. The United States Treasury will give you absolutely nothing for any of them except a replacement of another piece of paper. The substance, two billion ounces of silver and $25 billion in gold, that once backed these pieces of paper has disappeared. But you say, "Look at the great productivity of the United States. In its productivity lies its wealth." You are right.

Federal Debt of the United States in Billions of Dollars

Term	Years	Total Debt	Growth Rate
36 years	1879–1915	2 billion	Stable
16 years	1916–1932	18 billion	1 billion per year
10 years	1932–1942	71 billion	5.3 billion per year
10 years	1942–1952	260 billion	19 billion per year
10 years	1952–1962	348 billion	8.8 billion per year
10 years	1962–1972	442 billion	9.4 billion per year
2 years	1972–1974	495 billion	21.5 billion per year

Federal debt stayed steady at 2 billion from 1875 to 1915—40 years
Federal debt grew 250 billion 1870 to 1945—75 years
Federal debt grew 250 billion 1945 to 1975—30 years.

Did you stop to think that this productivity does not belong to the government? Rather to the people. That the vast scores and hundred of billions spent by the government has been collected from the people and that the government gave the people IOUs. The IOUs are government bonds and they are the currency.

The government alone owes this money, and the government has nothing in its vaults to back it up.

Say the government sold a billion dollars of 30-year bonds in 1930. In 1960 it sells $3 billion worth of 30-year bonds. It uses one billion to pay off the original buyers of 1930. It borrows the other two billion to work with. The newly borrowed two billion will be paid off 30 years from now *if* the people of the United States 30 years from now still trust the government enough to buy more bonds. If they don't trust the government the present lenders will get nothing.

The government does not have anything in its vaults with which to pay off its debts.

The government has never repaid the money it spent and lent for World War II. It just borrowed from U.S. citizens and then borrowed again (bonds) when bills came due. So what you have is debt money. It circulates mostly by force. It is called "lawful money" and "legal tender." Did anyone every have to write those assurances on a silver dollar or $20 gold piece?

The truth is that, regardless of any laws, your savings account in the bank is a debt of the U.S. government. The $10 bill in your pocket is a debt. If people quit lending, if they rebel at more oppressive taxes, this money will disappear. Because it is only a debt. It is really nothing.

When this will happen you may judge as well as I. But happen it will.

Debt money is the product of the new era—the new age—that began with the Bretton Woods agreement of 1944. The reason the government

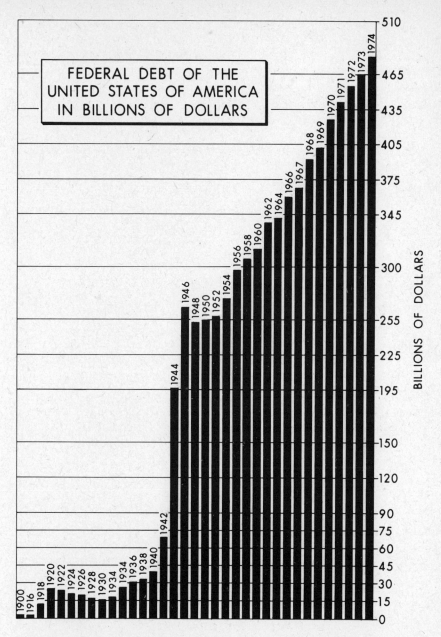

FEDERAL DEBT OF THE UNITED STATES OF AMERICA IN BILLIONS OF DOLLARS

BILLIONS OF DOLLARS

This graph shows the extremely small and stable debt condition of the U.S. in the first part of the century, its dramatic initial growth after the establishment of the Federal Reserve Bank in 1914, and the phenomenal pyramid that has arisen and continues to rise.

No tree grows to the sky and neither will this one. When it falls, so will the fiat currency that it represents.

did not have to pay off the cost of World War II was that it borrowed most of the savings of all the people and paid the bills with that. But having done so, it still owed the people in the form of bonds and fiat currencies. It has never paid the people—except to borrow from new generations to pay off the old generations. It is operating because all of the people of the United States *believe* that a debt bearing the signature of the government is as good as gold—or at least as good as U.S. money.

But it is not.

The United States government operates like our imaginary Howard Hughes who has squandered all his assets but still operates because people believe his IOUs are good. But remember, Howard Hughes' IOUs are just as good as real money as long as people *believe* that Howard Hughes still has his assets. When they find out he does not, the Hughes money collapses.

So the prosperity following World War II ushered in an era of plentiful money. Truly, Jacques Rueff hit it on the nose when he called it the era of inflation.

The money was sent to Europe, and the same money was spent in America, and all the savings of the people that had been collected in bonds and taxes were used, and have now been consumed.

The era that was launched in 1945 increasingly encouraged, as it progressed, the expansion of credit. If people were to save and pay off their debts, they would buy fewer washing machines, automobiles, etc. This in turn would cause a slowdown in the factories. This could bring on unemployment. Unemployment would result in the default of debts and in seizures of property. If that process ever got started people would sell out of the stock market, producing a crash, margins would be called, and more stock market sales would be necessitated. The whole monetary process would go into reverse.

Once launched upon this era of inflation, the only salvation was to keep it going. Each year the interest on the national debt was mounting until by 1973 the interest required nearly $24 billion of Mr. Nixon's $257 billion budget, and well over $30 billion on Mr. Ford's $350 billion budget of 1975.

The meaning of all this is that the debt continues to build astronomically on a foundation that was never meant to carry it, and that is now cracking and caving in under the enormous weight. The money supply must keep on increasing, even if only to pay the interest. Never mind a thought of paying off the principal. That by now has become forever impossible.

All this means that the money supply will have to continue to increase to avoid the dreaded bust. But it means that the dreaded bust will not be avoided.

12

CHANGED PEOPLE IN A NEW ERA

The tremendous flood of money couldn't help but have its consequences upon the social structure and the basic attitudes of the people. They jubilantly welcomed the era. But it was not their fault. The people did not understand what was going on. How could they? The government and the press assured them that humanity was now launched into a new age when there would be plenty for all. So confident were the policy makers that they had discovered the endless fountain of money, they even passed a law called the Unemployment Act. It prohibited unemployment, as if the government had so much power that it could actually prescribe the degree of prosperity of the country.

It was a testimonial to man's puffed-up image of himself as the Lord of the Earth. He had forgotten that man was a recent arrival and that nature wouldn't pay the slightest attention to his silly pronouncements.

But the people believed that they were living in a changed world—and they became a changed people.

And why not! Whereas once you had to lay out substantial cash (savings) to buy a car, now you were urged to buy one with no down payment at all. Whereas once you had to pay it off in a year, now you could pay it off in as much as two or three years. Whereas once you had to have 50 percent for the price of a bungalow, now you needed only

10 percent. And finally, by 1972, if you had $500 you could buy a $20,000 house with $500. But by early 1975 you were not able to buy any house at all, because the savings and loans associations had no money. The chicken was coming home to roost.

Up to then the mortgage companies had been happy to lend the money. Why not? After all, wasn't there a law that said that unemployment had been banished—just as King Arthur had banished snow from Camelot. That being so, no mortgagee would ever be without work, or at least enough social security to make his payments.

As a consequence the generation that became teenagers in the late fifties and early sixties were brought up to believe that credit was a desirable way of life. They were brought up to have what they wanted now, and pay later; whereas earlier generations had been taught to save first and buy when they had the money. What a drastic change! It was insidious as it developed, and it came about almost unnoticed.

Then young people were led to believe that the state owed them not only a living but also an education.

Those who didn't want to work found that they could do almost as well on unemployment insurance. Their weekly checks of course, were being paid by those who were willing to work. Any surplus unemployment contributions went into the government coffers in Washington. But this money was not saved. It was written off as a debt of the government and the money spent for other things, including Vietnam or other social benefits. Even these savings were quickly turned into debt.

Millions of workers set aside each week a portion of their earnings in the form of pensions for their old age. But this money was not saved either. This money was invested. The pension funds themselves bought government bonds, which are debt instruments. Those pensioners will eventually lose all or most, unless the government can later on continue to sell bonds to pay off the savings it has already consumed.

This new era of inflation made a business of selling debts, along the same lines as Proctor & Gamble made a business of selling soap.

"Why pay now, when you can pay later?" The credit card business mushroomed. Banks advertised to get you to accept their credit cards, so you could run an overdraft without worry. You could borrow on a heavier scale with this particular bank, and defer payment longer than you could with some other bank.

Private debt spiraled in sympathy with the public debt, and both hit astronomical levels. Under the social climate of the era of inflation no one saw anything wrong with this. The public tended to welcome it. After all, wages were constantly going up as the inflation contined. And prices were constantly going up. This was a great boom for the man who owed. If he had contracted a debt ten years ago, the constant inflation very materially trimmed the amount of his debt. Ten years ago a plumber, let's say, was earning $5 an hour and he borrowed $500 to pay for kitchen utilities for his wife. Now he earns $10 an hour and kitchen utilities have doubled in price. The debtor is always and forever paying off his debt with cheaper money.

But it must be a natural law that someone is losing.

The age of inflation sponsored a philosophy of immorality. We recall how the counterfeiters of Freedonia stole from the collective society when they made bogus money. They lived well, and got something for nothing. The price was paid by the *rest of the society*. When the counterfeiting was made *legal* by the printing of bogus money, the immorality was not reduced. The *theft* was just as real. Only the beneficiaries were different.

On November 1, 1972, I wrote the following column as a "Quiet Corner" in *Myers' Finance & Energy:*

When you come to the subject of inflation, the whole unprincipled fraternity of economists and government and banks are quite ready to condone it, if it doesn't raise its head too far. The popular theme over the last five years: "We've got to learn to live with inflation."

Perhaps five percent a year is too much, but three percent a year is acceptable.

Now these same men will instantly agree that inflation is a thief. For safekeeping you put your money with these bankers. But while you sleep, and throughout every hour of your sleep, the thief is peeling it off. If you have a million dollars in the bank, five percent inflation robs you of fifty thousand dollars in the course of a year. Every month you have lost four thousand dollars. Every night of the month the thief has walked off with a hundred and thirty dollars. Now they tell us it would be all right if he only walked off with fifty dollars. *Learn to live with him!*

You make a deal with a thief to live with you forever. Since he is a thief, you know full well that his ambition will constantly grow. You know at the beginning that you will end a pauper.

Yet, our middle-headed monetary seers preach to us: "Live with *acceptable* inflation." *COMPROMISE.*

Certain laws served mankind for thousands of years. Without these laws there could have been no social order. The ten commandments were not really new to Moses. In different form they were essential to the existence of the most primitive society. Thou shalt not steal. Can you half steal? Thou shalt not covet thy neighbor's wife. Can you half covet her? Would you like to have her, and still not covet her? Thou shalt not commit adultery. Can you partly commit adultery? Thou shalt not kill. We use the term "half-kill" but it's a misnomer. You can gravely injure someone, but either you kill him or you don't.

So it goes. Can you be fifty percent honest? To be half honest is to be dishonest. How far would you like to trust a man whom you know to be seventy-five percent honest? I say that every politician who would condone a three percent inflation is an unprincipled man; and he is a dishonest man, because he is quite prepared to accept the thesis that a *little stealing is alright.* No society can survive without the law: Thou shalt not steal.

Inflation is *monetary sin.* Virtue refuses to mix with it. Virtue and sin are repulsive one to another.

So the era of inflation involved more than money. It involved a deterioration of the fibers of morality. When a society becomes immoral, stealing is countenanced. Plunder is made legal. Plunder is respected.

We have seen from our society of Freedonia that the entire social structure will fall unless men can be secure in the knowledge that they can retain what they have earned. Undermine the sacred right of private property and the right to retain it, and you have struck a blow at morality. And you have proclaimed, "Let us all plunder one another!"

The age of inflation produced a dry rot that began to destroy the timbers under the social structure soon after the ending of World War II. By 1973 the timbers under the economy were rotten. Still the building stood. Still the building looked beautiful. And those who did not wish to know about the timbers and the foundation, refused to cast their eyes at the base of the building. They only looked at the beautiful painted walls and the great shining glass windows, and they said, "All is good. Look at the building. What a beautiful building we have built!"

In other words the age of inflation, having produced a public immorality, is guaranteed its extension by this immorality until it falls down of its own weight. For a trend, once securely in motion, does not stop of its own accord. Its own accumulated poisons stop it.

Henry George, a thinker far ahead of his time, wrote in 1879 in his book *Progress and Poverty:* "For in social development, as in everything else, motion tends to persist in straight lines, and therefore where there has been a previous advance, it is extremely difficult to recognize decline. Even when it has fully commenced there is an almost irresistible tendency to believe that the forward movement, which has been advancing and is still going on, is still advancing." George also believed that the moral breakdown of society started from the top and he said:

"The most ominous political sign is the growth of a sentiment which either doubts the existence of an honest man in public office or looks on him as a fool for not seizing his opportunities. That is to say, the people themselves are becoming corrupted."

The nonchalance with which the public at first accepted the Watergate bugging suggests deterioration. The lack of moral indignation regarding deceitful and immoral practices fit comfortably into the picture of a public that is quite content to condone the immorality of inflation; and likewise its cousins—cheating and lying and spying. The public itself would have been quite content to forget Watergate.

Tonight, as I write these words, I see on television a housewife being interviewed in a supermarket, and she is asked if she believes the claims of the advertisers. She replies quite frankly, "Of course not. It's quite an accepted fact that they just make those claims to sell more products."

Politicians are no longer expected to be scrupulously honest. Until the time of Watergate they were regarded as foolish if they didn't take advantage of some of their opportunities.

Inflation has destroyed the old-fashioned virtue of thrift. Why save if what you save will constantly evaporate? It has destroyed the old-fashioned virtue of ambition, for why work harder when the man next to you lags behind and earns exactly the same amount as you do? It has destroyed the idea of pay as you go, for those who pay as they go are the suckers; those who pay later pay off with cheaper dollars.

And of course this could not have happened in a short period of time. The gold-exchange standard of 1923 to 1934 did not produce an immorality in the population. That could only happen over the course of a generation or more, which Jacques Rueff has rightly called the age of inflation.

And since inflation will not stop of its own accord, and since it cannot be stopped except at the cost of a deflation, its continuation is certain until it brings about a collapse of the economy and a collapse of social order. As 1976 dawned, the structure was beginning to tremble.

All of this has been evident for some time. It could be told by the criteria as outlined by Henry George when he said: "Civilization has begun to wane when, in proportion to population, we must build more and more prisons, more and more alms houses, more and more insane asylums.

WHAT THIS MEANS TO YOU

It means that violence and crime will increase. It means that life in the large cities will grow more hazardous. In the most congested areas it will mean staying home at night, and it will mean the necessity of better locks on your doors, all-around increased personal security, and increased vigilance.

It means that you should prepare yourself mentally and emotionally to meet these perils.

From a practical standpoint it means that you should expect a temporary breakdown in the distribution system. The productive capacity of the United States is totally adequate, but distribution is vulnerable because of the physical dangers threatening the personnel. For instance, trucks might be looted and truck drivers might refuse to man the trucks until order had been restored. Because of that you should accumulate all of the necessities to tide you over at least a 90-day period. These should all be of an imperishable nature. If the projection is wrong, you have lost nothing, but if the projection is right, you will be mighty thankful for your foresight.

You should teach yourself and your children a new self-sufficiency and the development of hobbies that can give you an enjoyment of life not dependent upon the now generally accepted forms of amusement.

13

INTERNATIONAL TENTACLES

The reader is bound to have reached a stage by now where he will be wondering rather urgently how much longer this inflation will continue, when it will come to an end, how it will come to an end, and what, if anything, he can do to protect himself—not only from the economic repercussions of the collapse of inflation, but also from the social consequences of the economic collapse. To attempt even an intelligent *guess* in answer to these questions it is necessary to understand the international implications.

It is the international aspects of inflation that have allowed it to thrive so long, and the length of its life will be found to have been an important determinant of the severity of the collapse and the duration of the collapse.

Never before in history was inflation able to indure for such a lengthy period. Never in history did it encompass the world. The reason is that never before in history did we have a gold-exchange standard, at first condoned and then, of necessity, supported by the world. Previously the jaws of inflation frequently crushed a single country. Never before were the jaws so huge that they could grip the globe.

The greatest currency the world has known—the greatest lubricant for industry and trade and prosperity—was the British pound. Its widespread use encircled the world, but that was the gold standard. During the age of the gold standard, inflation was never able to raise its head more than an inch before it was knocked down again.

But when all of the countries of the free world endorsed the gold-exchange standard in 1944, they set the stage for the most massive fall in the history of man—a fall that would make the very gods tremble. When all the countries set their sails by the U.S. dollar, the flotilla had embarked on a voyage into the sea of oblivion.

It worked this way:

The reserves of a country represent its profit position. They are like the savings of a man. They are a guard against a rainy day. If the crops are bad in the country, the reserves can be called upon to buy imports. So the reserves of a country are extremely important.

When the reserves of a country are the currency of another country, the first country becomes necessarily dependent upon the health of the second. The United States dollar became the reserve currency of the world. Holdings of United States dollars became the protection of those countries against a rainy day. If the dollar was durable those piggy bank savings were secure. The value of the reserves of other countries would vary according to the value of the United States dollar.

Once the countries of the world included masses of United States dollars in their reserves, it was to their interest to preserve the integrity of the dollar. They had been trapped into a position where they had to save the dollar to save their own necks.

France was the first country to see that the dollar was so far gone it would eventually have to tumble. The French logic was that if the dollar will have to tumble, better it tumble early than late. For the longer the deterioration of the dollar continues, the worse will be the plight of everyone when it falls.

General DeGaulle, in the mid-sixties, with unerring vision, started a policy of changing French reserves from dollars into gold. Some may blame him for contributing to the fall of the dollar. That would be foolish. A currency falls because it is sick of itself. Had the dollar been sound it would simply have shrugged off this paltry attack.

Unfortunately for the world, DeGaulle was thwarted by internal problems in France in May of 1969. His efforts to establish a solid base for world money had to be abandoned. Thereafter the weakening paper giant was propped up again, fed some more stimulant, and pushed out into the arena looking better than ever.

DeGaulle saw that the constant increase of debts of the United States was a trend in motion that would likely continue. He observed what was plain for anyone to see, that the debts of the United States well exceeded the gold supply. Everyone knew that the world's monetary system was based on the idea that any outstanding dollars could always, without question, be changed to gold. DeGaulle saw that this day was nearly over. He knew that it was only a question of time until the nations would clamor for gold for their dollars. He also knew that by that time the United States would have manufactured so many more dollars that the situation, when it came eventually to crisis, would be infinitely worse.

To understand fully the development of international unconfidence one must go back to 1961. For sixteen years—since Bretton Woods—the United States alone had guaranteed the gold validity of its outstanding dollars. But in that year, when the debt exceeded the gold, the public of the world became alarmed and began to trade dollars for gold at a premium, yielding $41 for an ounce of gold in place of the $35 guaranteed maximum price by the United States. The United States had to call for help. It asked the major nations to deposit a large amount of gold into a joint pool, and jointly to inform the world that all of these big countries would stand behind the price of gold at $35, and would sell gold in unlimited quantity to all takers. These nations, already holding sizable numbers of dollars, and hoping for its stability—even France—gladly cooperated. The free market price of gold dropped back to $35.

But the sickness was inherent, although it was progressing slowly. By 1968 the United States gold supply had dwindled to about $10 billion, and the debts had risen to well over $30 billion. The demand for gold all over the world was growing. Still the gold pool sold to all corners. But there was a hemorrhage of gold, and it was becoming alarming. Realistically, France perceived that in the market place of the world, under free conditions, an ounce of gold was worth more than $35. France dropped out of the gold pool. Although this was kept secret, the run on gold continued.

The internal paper currency of the United States amounted to about $40 billion, and there was a law that said that this currency had to be backed 25 percent by gold. That meant that the entire remaining U.S. gold stock of $10 billion was committed to the pocket currency in circulation. There was need also to increase the pocket currency. The United States was at an impasse. It could not print any more folding money unless it increased the price of gold, for it only had about $10 billion in gold and it had $40 billion in outstanding currency. That would mean the devaluation of the dollar against gold—in other words, an increase in the price of gold. But that would greatly undermine confidence internationally.

President Lyndon Johnson and Secretary of the Treasury Henry Fowler thought that if they removed the gold from behind the circulating greenbacks it would do two things. It would let them print unlimited currency; and it would shore up international confidence because they could make the whole $10 billion available to foreign central banks. With new gold available, the fears about the dollar would abate despite the fact the the United States owed three or four times as much as its total store of gold. So President Johnson urged the Congress to pass a law that would remove the gold backing from the paper currency inside the United States. At one time the paper currency had been 100 percent backed by gold, later 50 percent, later 33 percent. Now even the 25 percent backing had to be abandoned.

What greater signal to the international monetary world that the dollar was sinking? Foreign treasuries were publicly uncritical; they didn't want to say anything to undermine the dollar because their own savings were almost wholly in dollars.

The demand for gold was cured only briefly. By March 1968 there was such a run on gold that the United States Treasury had to throw in the towel. All the markets of the world were closed while the heads of the central banks and finance ministers met in Washington to decide what to do. Unless the dollar was held to be convertible into gold, the Bretton Woods agreement was in ruins. Then what would they use for a monetary system? Then what would be the value of the stored dollars in the reserves of the various countries—their protection against a rainy day? It was to the interest of them all to support any move that seemed reasonable to preserve the status of the dollar. That was the invention of the two-tier gold system.

But a two-level price for anything is in direct contradiction of all natural law. A price is a level at which a commodity will trade back and forth—where the buyer is willing to pay the amount for which the seller will release the goods. There never can be two real prices. One must be an artificial or enforced price. It is, therefore, the weaker price because it is the unrealistic price. It will, therefore, sooner or later collapse. The two-tier gold system was a further signal of the desperate straits of the dollar.

But countries hoped against hope that it would work so that their own reserves of dollars would be protected in their value. The gold-exchange standard had got them into this trap. There was no visible way out.

Their greatest wish was that the United States would cure its balance of payments problem. This may at first sound complicated, but it is extremely simple. The balance of payments is just like your bank account. If, at the end of a year, you have managed to save some money you have a balance in your bank account. If, at the end of a year, you have spent more than you have earned, your bank account has declined from last year's figure, or you have gone into debt and you have red ink.

Not since 1950, except for the year 1957, has the United States produced a positive balance at the end of the year. It has always spent more. There was some defense for this: it was said that the United States was keeping armies in Europe for the protection of the European countries against communism; the United States was fighting communism in Asia; the United States provided the nuclear umbrella, and so forth. Excuse after excuse was used as reason for the poor balance of payments showing.

Each and every year, from 1960, the U. S. Treasury officials had predicted that the following year would show a great improvement. Each new year would see the weaknesses of the past overcome and the turnabout would be at hand. The other nations wished desperately to believe this.

During the years 1967 to 1972 I was in Europe several times and talked to some of the authorities, particularly in Germany and Switzerland. It was obvious they were clinging to a wish that was being paraded as a belief. On each occasion they staunchly maintained that the United States was curing its balance of payments. The United States is the greatest industrial nation in the world. You see it has a good surplus of trade. That shows its essential health. For many years it has been earning $5 billion in surplus trade.

But 1970 was a year of horror. In that year trade barely balanced. And 1971 was a year of disaster. Trade went into the red and the United States bought $2 billion more than it sold in goods. The year 1972 was a cataclysm. The trade deficit increased to $6 billion. In 1973 there was a small surplus, but again in 1974 a trade deficit of nearly $6 billion.

Externally between trade deficit and other spending, the U. S. seemed to be on a course of about $12 billion a year deficit.

By the year 1974 external debts of the United States would exceed $100 billion; the total reserves of all the countries in the world including the United States are only about $150 billion. In other words, the U. S. debt approached the saved reserves of all the countries in the world, including itself.

And half of the reserves of all of the countries in the world was in the form of U.S. dollars. Their savings were largely U.S. debts.

No wonder there was panic on the international monetary fronts.

In face of the true facts, Nixon's ravings against the speculators who were ruining the dollar was exposed as a weak-faced and bare-faced lie. One might as well blame the expectant undertaker for the patient's death as blame the speculators for the plight of the dollar.

But it is necessary to go back a step. The two-tier gold system of 1968, with Herculean cooperation by other nations, held the dollar for nearly three years. That was because the other nations agreed that even though they had the right, under Bretton Woods, to claim gold for the dollars in their treasuries, they would not claim it. They also agreed not even to buy any gold. They agreed further not to sell any gold. Among them they had *isolated* gold on the official monetary market in the vain hope that the free market price would fall to the artificial market price of $35 an ounce. If this could be accomplished, the theoretical value of their national reserves in their piggy banks could be maintained. If gold got away, Bretton Woods would be smashed and their reserves would shrink. For 20 or 30 years they had been counting on the stability of the U.S. dollar as a store of value.

In order to keep gold from charging out of the stockade and smashing the monetary practices of world trade, gold had somehow to be discredited. The inventiveness of the U.S. Treasury was without limit.

Why not have an international reserve that had nothing to do with gold? Get the story around that this would be the new world money, and people would sell their gold. The Central Banks of course wouldn't sell an ounce, but the hope was that the foolish public would sell its gold. The idea was to get the public to think along these lines: If the banks won't pay anything for our gold—won't buy it all—we will find ourselves owning a dead horse. The price will go to next to nothing. What good is gold—really? Let's get out while we can!!

Thus the authorities, in the true spirit of the con men on the Mississippi River boats of old, would persuade the suckers into releasing the only enduring money they had, while the con men would pick it up for themselves later on—cheap.

Sometimes laymen are smarter than experts. The laymen of the world felt that if gold was cherished by the Central Banks to the point where they wouldn't part with any of their own, gold must be all right. Many said to themselves, "As long as it's good enough for the banks, it's good enough for me."

An example of the propaganda of those days was in a report by Pierre Rinfret on November 28, 1969. As an instance of the type of economists who have been listened to by the masses—this is too good to miss:

> In 1967, I had lunch with a high official of the Bank of England. When I suggested that if gold were freed it might go to fifty dollars, the lofty official laughed. "You don't know anything about the price of gold! Give us two years and we'll smash the price to twenty-five dollars an ounce."

The Rinfret letter goes on:

> The luminary from the Bank of England explained: "The central banks will stop buying gold. The moment they do that, South Africa will have lost her market. Then there must be a free market. If the central banks refused to buy, South Africa will have to sell on the free market. Since she depends upon gold exports, she will have to sell it all there.

"Now remember there is no floor anymore. People who bought at thirty-five dollars can't be sure they'll get thirty-five dollars. The central banks will then step in and with one billion dollars of gold will smash the price to twenty-five dollars. We're professional; we can beat the amateurs at their own game any day of the week. But here's the beautiful part. When we get the price down to twenty-five dollars an ounce, and all the gold that's been locked away comes out, we central bankers step in and buy at bargain prices.

"We'll have taught the amateurs a lesson they won't soon forget. We will have stabilized the world monetary system. Just watch us. We're going to do it."

So much for this shallow-minded dreamer so high in the Bank of England. More importantly, what was Mr. Rinfret's considered judgment of this opinion?

"The truth is," he said in his letter of November 28, 1969, "the central bankers now have control, and are having their own way. The first thing to realize is that they may drive the price down to twenty-five dollars an ounce." One wonders what Mr. Rinfret's comments were on this point in late 1974 when gold sold for $200 an ounce.

The Special Drawing Rights or paper-gold, as it was called, was to be the magic formula for monetary reform. The authorities did not seem to be bothered by the fact that Special Drawing Rights were unadulterated hot air. S.D.R.s were *declared* to be money. We were back to the days of Kublai Khan.

But we have seen from our examination of the state of Freedonia that real money is a warehouse receipt, and as such is in itself wealth, and that the precious metals are only a measurement of that wealth. They are the Fairbanks Morse scale. They were registering short weight on the beefsteak. So the authorities denounced the scale. The trouble, they said, is not a shortage of beefsteak but the tyranny of this old-fashioned scale. Smash the scale. Demonetize gold!

By now by the invention of, and as a result of, the gold-exchange standard, inflation was threatening to swamp the world. The only answer the authorities could come up with was more inflation—this time *international* inflation (S.D.R.s) in addition to the national monetary inflation (the dollar).

14

SPECIAL DRAWING RIGHTS— THE ULTIMATE DELUSION

The name itself—paper gold—was a brazen admission that it was a fake. Soon it became the butt of jokes. In my newsletters I referred to it frequently in the same breath with glass diamonds, virgin prostitutes, etc. The authorities became rather sensitive about the derision being heaped on their latest monetary protege, and they began to restrict official reference to Special Drawing Rights rather than paper gold.

That at least sounded prestigious, and carried the implication that it was the brilliant creation of some very highly qualified monetary wizards.

Alas, even a cursory examination of this name showed it to be an accurate description of yet another farce. For Special Drawing Rights must certainly be *special rights* to draw—obviously special rights to *borrow*.

The new world money, then, was once again not money at all; it was a right to *borrow* money. But what money? It was nothing more than a right to create additional international debt. A new engine to be added to the era of inflation to blow the balloon bigger.

Western civilization—the common man—shrugged its shoulders; slumbered on.

By 1972 nations had issued, in all, about $9 billion of these rights for countries to borrow, and these S.D.R.s were mixed in with all of the rest of the reserves in the Central Banks. They were rated to have exactly the same value in dollars as an ounce of gold. In other words, a thing called an S.D.R.—a goose egg—was *declared* to be worth one/ thirty-fifth of an ounce of gold. If you had, as a Central Bank, 35 million of these goose eggs then you had a million ounces of gold. It was one and the same thing—based on the theory of Kublai Khan.

It was as if you had declared to your neighbor on the farm that three pieces of shavings were worth one egg; and as if you said to your neighbor, "I now give you 36 pieces of shavings, please give me one dozen eggs."

This is oversimplified but it is absolutely true, and the monetary authorities thought they could pull it off. Unbelievable!

By the end of 1972 several important countries were beginning to have reservations about the ability of the authorities to sustain this fantasy; and at the end of 1972 they refused to issue any further Special Drawing Rights. The curtain was beginning to descend on this the most nonsensical monetary idea ever conceived by man.

What had happened, to that point, was merely that the reserves of all of the Central Banks had been diluted a further $9 billion. More water in the whisky.

If the gold-exchange standard was an engine of inflation, the Special Drawing Rights were an inflationary engine with a four-barrel carbure- tor. To all sane men it must have foretold acceleration on the road to inflationary disaster—not for one country, but for the world.

By mid-1972, the concept was privately being recognized for what it was—a ridiculous farce. In the press it was still being occasionally touted as the magic new solution for world monetary reform. In the highest inner offices, however, sober bankers shook their heads, and began to see at last that, if there were an ultimate in the monetary land of delusion, surely S.D.R.s were it.

Delusion grows from illusion, and illusion grows from a wish. One pertinent thing about an illusion is that it is quite real as long as it persists. The difference between an illusion and reality is simple. The illusion, being unreal, always collapses; and reality, being real, survives forever. Sometimes it is hard to distinguish between illusion and reality, because, while illusion exists, it works just as well as reality.

The second pertinent thing about illusion is that it is an "all or nothing" deal. That is, it either exists completely, or it evaporates com- pletely. When reality has been overrated there is something left. When illusion is exploded there is *nothing* left.

This makes mass illusion very dangerous. When a whole nation or a group of nations come to believe in an illusion, the return to reality is so sharp, so abrupt, that it leaves no time for adjustment. An exposed illusion wilts before your eyes. Persistent illusions suffered by individuals are called "delusions." Delusions are the mark of insanity. They may be delusions of grandeur or of anything else that is not true—or not real. But to the victim the delusion is absolutely true—absolutely real; and given the premise of this delusion, all of the actions of the victim are logical. Take the premise away, and his actions are insane.

When an entire people get hung up on a persistent illusion, it becomes a delusion; and you have mass madness. Every so often the world goes mad. Common sense becomes nonsense. The crusades were utter madness. They had no real purpose, but they persisted through generations.

World War I was madness. Today no real reason can be found for it. The tulipomania in seventeenth-century Holland was wild economic madness. Fortunes were paid for a single tulip bulb. The delusion was that tulip bulbs were valuable and that they would continue to increase in value, no matter what. Finally someone came to his senses and asked himself just who really must positively own a tulip bulb?—no matter how pretty the tulips. And that man sold!

The crowd was at last awakened, recognizing that there was after all no *real* value to tulip bulbs, except to a gardener. The crash that followed the tulipomania was the worst to that point in history. There were numerous others.

During these periods of mass insanity the delusion works quite well. The danger of the delusion is not in staying in it, but coming out of it.

Western civilization has been operating under a mass credit delusion. It is the delusion that "*nothing* will substitute for *something*"—"paper is as good as gold." The meaning is that a token is just as good as the real thing. The meaning is that a picture of you has as much reality as you. Carry the delusion further and the madman declares that the picture is the real thing and you derive your existence only because of the existence of the picture.

Expressed in terms of the deluded U.S. economists, it went this way: the dollar does not depend on gold or the value of gold. Gold only gets its value because the U.S. Treasury has been willing to pay $35 an ounce for it. Take away that willingness and gold is worth nothing. Gold derives its value by virtue of the reflection of gold on the millions of paper notes. Value therefore rests in these reflections—rather than the substance reflected. You enjoy your physical reality by virtue of a photograph of you.

Following this delusion, all backing having been removed from the U.S. domestic dollar and, finally, from the U.S. international dollar, the madness was expanded to embrace an international mechanism of S.D.R.s that were declared to have a gold value—although no one in the world would give any gold for an S.D.R.

Still such a mechanism can work for a while. The tulips of yesteryear *were valuable* so long as people had confidence that the tulips had that value, and believed that other people had the same confidence. The same went for the dollar for a time, even after the backing had been removed.

The S.D.R. was not different.

Here is a little satire I wrote about the S.D.R. in *Myers' Finance & Energy* of December 16, 1971.

DONUT HOLES

A One Act Play

Starring

Richard Nixon	Karl Schiller	Valery d'Estaing
Arthur Burns		John Connally

Nixon: Gentlemen, I have called this meeting because of a devastating crisis. As you know, we have run out of gold, and we have had to lay our bets on S.D.R.s. But the plain fact is, S.D.R.s are not catching on! Arthur Burns has come up with a new idea. Arthur—tell them.

Arthur Burns: The thinking is, gentlemen, that S.D.R.s are too vague. People can't imagine an S.D.R. You've got to have something they can visualize. At the same time it must be something which is nothing. Because if it is something, we shall be restricted in our creation of money. What I'm going to say may sound foolish at first. It did to me, when I read it in a Canadian financial letter. But don't laugh, gentlemen, I propose we rename S.D.R.s, and that from now on they be known officially throughout the world as DONUT HOLES.

Schiller: Whatever the Americans say is acceptable to the Germans. We have already upvalued twice to assist the U.S. Treasury at considerable sacrifice to our people. After all, we started the war, and we deserve to suffer—even if you get the donuts and we only get the holes.

Burns: Suffering will be unnecessary. Our international debts will be denominated in Donut Holes. Each Donut Hole is worth one thirty-fifth of an ounce of gold—exactly the same as an S.D.R. All S.D.R.s will be converted into Donut Holes. Now this has the advantage of giving people the illusion of reality. When you think of a Donut Hole, what do you think of? A donut, of course! Maybe even a cup of coffee. But an S.D.R. lacks this. I am suggesting that the world monetary system should operate on Donut Holes.

D'Estaing: France will go along with the idea only if you agree to use real donuts in order to get the holes.

Connally: The U.S. will not be crucified on a cross of donuts. We are going to de-emphasize the donuts and emphasize the holes. And we are going to use the holes, and that's the end of it! And that hole is worth one thirty-fifth of an ounce of gold—the same as an S.D.R. And that is what we *say* it is worth, so that is what it is worth. In the matter of international balances we will store all the Donut Holes in a single building. Each country will have his man in this building, with a rake, and as the balances change, the piles of Donut Holes will be raked into the bins of the respective countries.

Nixon: I got an idea on that. At the California White House we have these Japanese bamboo rakes. They're not very strong, but they would handle voluminous quantities of Donut Holes.

Connally: Yes, but what about your quota on Jap rakes?

Nixon: I forgot that. By Jove!

Connally: There is no need to use Japanese products. In Texas we have ten-prong pitchforks. They have proved their worth in handling the products of Texas, and they can be washed off for use by the IMF.

Nixon: I agree, we should buy American. I will arrange tax rebates for factories producing these forks. This will create jobs, and we will sell the forks to the IMF for moving Donut Holes.

Schiller: Germany agrees. Even if every German is out of work, I agree. Hitler started the war, and we deserve to pay. Let no one try to stop Germany from making its just retribution.

D'Estaing: France agrees that the Donut Hole is worth every bit as much as the S.D.R. We further agree that a Donut Hole is better than an S.D.R. because it gives the illusion of something real, while the S.D.R. concept could well return us to the middle ages, when the debate raged: "How many angels can dance on the point of a needle?" If we use S.D.R.s, our economists will surely begin to argue: "How many billion S.D.R.s can be stored in the eye of a needle?" But if we use Donut Holes, the question will not arise, because Donut Holes have a diameter of about one inch each. Nevertheless, France will never agree to just the holes—unless we also have the donuts.

Nixon: The perversity of France is obstructing monetary progress. I hereby declare that the United States recognizes Donut Holes as the sole international world currency. Each Donut Hole is worth one thirty-fifth of an ounce of gold and is instantly transferable into an S.D.R. And all dollars are convertible immediately into either S.D.R.s or Donut Holes. They all have the same value. Nobody can argue with that.

Connally (aside to Burns): Do you think it's going to work?

Burns: It better work! You see, Donut Holes are about the only thing the United States doesn't owe.

Nevertheless the S.D.R. concept is not without value. The value lies in the concept of an international money—a money against which all money would be measured. This would mean that no country in the world would ever again be in a position to dominate the monetary scene with its national currency. All national settlements would revolve around the *value* of this international currency.

If all countries rated their money in S.D.R.s, *and if S.D.R.s were given a gold value and were convertible into gold at a realistic price* in terms of the various currencies so related, then the monetary system of the world would have a point on which to take a reading.

The S.D.R. could never be a true world money until it was redeemable for real goods or measured by a metal exchange. Thus the Special Drawing Right, as we understood it when it first came to be used, would turn out to be an entirely different animal. Its name would be obsolete. *The idea that a right to borrow money was tantamount to having money would have been exploded.* But the basic concept of an international money is something that may survive. It may be the cornerstone of a great advance for civilization—once we have come out of this "bad trip" of worldwide ethereal credit.

Here is some elementary substantiation that the S.D.R. concept was beginning to fall apart as early as the fall of 1972.

Karl Klassen, head of the German Central Bank, was asked if S.D.R.s ought to be based on gold. He replied:

"It would be premature to speculate as to whether or not S.D.R.s should be based on gold."

That was an immensely important statement from a central banker, because if S.D.R.s are to be based on gold, they are no longer Special Drawing Rights at all. They become real money. Not special, but universal. Not a drawing, but a deposit.

The ethereal becomes earthly. The spirit becomes a body. The ghost is banished.

So Mr. Klassen's answer amounted to this: It is too early to speculate that we ought to abandon the *concept* of reality as a backing for international currency.

That in itself was quite a blow to the whole "Alice in Wonderland" idea of imaginary money as a panacea for the monetary ills of the world.

France's D'Estaing had already said that S.D.R.s should be based on gold. When Klassen was asked to comment on this he thought that "D'Estaing had not over-emphasized the role of gold."

That was tantamount to an admission by two important countries that perhaps the S.D.R. as it was known should be scrapped and later changed into a different asset with a gold base. The U.S. press, either purposely or out of ignorance, quickly sluffed over these, the two most momentous statements about S.D.R.s since they had first been introduced.

In September 1972 Pierre-Paul Schweitzer had said that S.D.R.s should be kept but perhaps they should have a different name. But the name was already very descriptive—a highly accurate name. Could the head of the I.M.F. be implying that their nature should be changed?

For if the name were to be changed, wouldn't that be meant to reflect a change in the character of the S.D.R.?

In that case the new S.D.R. wouldn't be an S.D.R. at all. It would be a true international money backed by gold.

Following these statements by Klassen and others, the S.D.R. lost prestige throughout 1973, and by 1974 the term was seldom mentioned either by the monetarists or in the press. It would not be until the disturbing end of 1974, when the monetary authorities began to tremble in the face of a world recession, that they went back to the closet and again dragged out the S.D.R. for popular usage.

As an era of inflation ends, a new era may well be based on an international money convertible into gold, with the values of all currencies of the world described in terms of the international currency.

Because of the probable future enormous significance of the *concept,* a great deal of space has been taken up here with S.D.R.s. It is important for every man to understand just what the S.D.R. was originally and the monetary delusions on which it rested. As the mechanism of the S.D.R. may play a large role in our future, it is important to know what is being said as the news stories of the future refer to the "international currency"—whatever it may be called.

If you are a manager in a department store, a hairdresser, a bricklayer, or work on the assembly line at Ford, don't think that these subjects are too complicated for you. For money is quite simple. Only the gimmicks are complicated.

But don't you agree, after reading the above, that even the gimmicks, once they are exposed, are also as simple as a magician's trick—once you know how it is done?

15

MULTINATIONAL INFLATION THREATENS YOU

Most of us are too nonchalant about what is going on in the world of money. We are inclined to take the attitude: "This is too complicated for me."

Not at all. If you have a tenth-grade education you can understand it. It is the monetary authorities who make it *appear* complicated. It is my purpose here to clear away that hocus pocus. This book is written for you.

If you earn $10,000 a year and during the year you give out I.O.U.s totaling $12,000, and year after year for five years, you will find that your balance of payments is in deficit by $10,000. In other words, you owe $10,000 that you do not have. But this $10,000 is a claim on you and all your property. Your creditors are entitled to move in and sell your home, which is worth $20,000, and take their $10,000 and give you the balance—and then you must move into a new house half the size.

When the United States spends $10 billion a year in other parts of the world and in excess of what it sells and collects from other parts of the world, it has a balance of payments deficit of $10 billion. And if this goes on for five years it has a balance of payments deficit of $50 billion.

In the spring of 1973, Paul Volker, Under-Secretary of the U.S. Treasury, admitted that there were some $70 to $80 billion in foreign Central Banks, and about $10 to $20 billion more in other hands.

Just like your I.O.U.s, these dollars are I.O.U.s of the United States. You may ask how can that be? Aren't our dollars good?

When the monetary system of the gold-exchange standard was working, those I.O.U.s that the United States gave to other countries for goods and services, were returned to the United States Treasury—and the United States Treasury dished out the equivalent amount in gold—and the debt was paid!

That was all right as long as the gold lasted.

Once again to relate this to yourself: when you spend $1,000 a year more than your income for five years, presuming you had a bank account of $5,000, you could have absorbed that from your savings. You would have given up all your savings. But when your savings were gone (the U.S. gold pile), your I.O.U.s and your debts were irredeemable. It was no good for your creditors to come to your door with the I.O.U.s, you didn't have anything to pay them with. You had to slam the door on their fingers.

In August 1971 when President Nixon announced that the United States was breaking with gold, he slammed the teller's window on his creditors' fingers, the same as you slammed your door. The United States refused to redeem its I.O.U.s.

But some people felt that a U.S. dollar was still the mighty U.S. buck and it would still buy goods abroad, and so why should the foreigners be worried. The answer to this is also simple.

The normal reserves of Germany, for instance, were about $7 billion. About $4.5 billion of that had been gold and the other 2.5 billion was United States dollars that were "as good as gold" and redeemable for gold at the U.S. Treasury. By the spring of 1973 the German reserves were about $32 billion, and still only 4.5 billion was gold. The other $27-odd billion was sitting there. The question naturally arises—why not spend it somewhere else?

Well, the reserves of Japan were normally about $5 billion. By the spring of 1973 the reserves of Japan were $25 billion, and 23 billion of that was U.S. dollars, with less than one billion in gold. And so it went around the world.

If Germany wanted to buy from Japan, Japan would be very happy to take French francs or Dutch guilders that could be traded for anything in any country of the world—or gold—that would buy any currency anywhere in the world—but Japan did not want to take U.S. dollars because already it could not spend the U.S. dollars it had. Just as all your creditors would be fed up to the teeth with all your I.O.U.s that were no good to spend, so the national banks were chock full of dollars that no other national banks wanted.

But there is one point in all this that you might not have understood as a layman. When U.S. dollars went into Germany—for example, to buy goods or if U.S. citizens sent dollars into Germany to bank over there—those dollars had to be converted by the German Central Bank into German domestic currency. Look at the impact on the foreign country.

Germany's money supply was suddenly swollen to dangerous proportions that could break out in a ruinous wave of inflation. Try as they would to keep the extra funds in the Central Bank, those funds have a way of leaking out—and leaking out ever faster as they widen the hole in the dike. The countries of the world—banks and governments—were getting panicky. But what could they do to stop the dollars? If Volkswagen had sold half a million cars to the United States, the German authorities could hardly order Volkswagen not to pick up the payment in U.S. dollars and bring them home to convert into German marks to pay Volkswagen workers.

All kinds of foreign exchange controls were introduced, but they were no defense against the influx of dollars, as people around the world increasingly wanted to turn them in for some other currency. Huge U.S. corporations with operations in foreign countries scrambled to get rid of U.S. dollars so they would not lose their shareholders' money on an almost certain devaluation of the U.S. dollar.

President Nixon blamed the crises on the wicked speculators. Surely he knew better. He was well informed that confidence in the dollar—following his closure of the gold window—had crumbled.

But the point is that his outflow of dollars was spreading inflationary disease everywhere. Almost every country—including Switzerland—was now suffering an inflation greater than the United States as U.S. dollars swarmed in and were transformed into national currencies.

That is why you often heard the claim that the United States was *exporting* its inflation. While American authorities boasted that their inflation was less bad then elsewhere, U.S. dollars were causing the inflation in those other countries.

For example, if you get worried about the value of your U.S. dollars you may decide to convert them into Swiss francs and hold them in Switzerland. The Swiss try to stop you, as well as hordes of others.

If you had $5,000 in your bank account you felt would be safer in gold-backed Swiss francs, you would send this money to Zurich, where the Swiss bank would have to issue Swiss francs for your dollars. Multiply this to $5 billion and you can see why the Swiss government must issue the Swiss francs equivalent of $5 billion. If Switzerland had reserves of the equivalent $5 billion before, now it has $10 billion in the form of Swiss francs. How could the inflation invasion be stopped? The United States shrugged its shoulders and said, "That's your problem!"

This came to be known as dollar imperialism.

And that is how the whole world, in the spring of 1973, found itself in the grips of an inflation that it did not know how to control.

By the spring of 1975 Switzerland was charging 40-percent *negative* interest for the deposit of American money—mostly to no avail.

The reason is simple. Any central bank must issue its currency to another central bank. The Swiss sell Swiss watches. In order to use their money inside Switzerland they must have it in Swiss francs. Now, if France wants to buy watches from Switzerland, she would have to pay for these watches in Swiss francs. If the Central Bank of France offers French francs in Switzerland or on the money exchanges of the world, Switzerland must issue Swiss francs in exchange for the other currency —at the going rate—if it expects to sell anything. There is no way the Swiss national bank can avoid issuing a demand for francs.

All right—you want to change American dollars into Swiss francs. The Swiss say, "We will charge a 40-percent penalty per year for deposits in the form of Swiss francs in Switzerland." So you go to Amsterdam, or Vienna or some other place, and tell a bank you want to buy Swiss francs. The bank will order the Swiss francs from the Central Bank of Holland or Austria. Holland or Austria will present the dollars you have already changed into guilders or schillings and demand the Swiss francs from the Swiss government. Now you have a deposit of Swiss francs in Holland or Austria. The effort of the Swiss banks to block the transformation of American dollars into Swiss francs was futile.

And so every country in the world remains at the mercy of the inflowing dollars from the United States, which are acceptable on every exchange in the world at the going rate.

Therefore huge inflations in American dollars spread to other countries, which remain pretty much at the mercy of the Federal Reserve.

By the spring of 1973 confidence in the U.S. dollar had been shot. Two devaluations, a small one in December 1971 and a ten-percenter in February 1973, had set the stage for yet another fall.

Now the Arab countries were asking for further guarantees for oil. Some were saying they would rather leave it in the ground, where they knew it would retain its value, than sell it for U.S. dollars, the value of which was certain to depreciate. If they were going to sell it at all, they would raise the price.

The home-grown inflation of the U.S., spreading to other countries of the world, was beginning to come home to roost.

Nickel, cocoa, copper, chrome, coffee, timber, paper; all that vast array of raw materials—all of it—was going up in price. These prices were not subject to any U.S.-imposed price controls.

So it did affect you. And it will affect you. Whatever happens on the monetary fronts of the world will affect you. As the prices of the imported raw material rise in terms of U.S. dollars (as the dollar is devalued) you pay more in heat, in gas, in power, etc.

The effect of all this is to reduce your standard of living—like it or not.

Higher prices—more inflation—higher prices—bust—that's the scenario.

I hope the previous chapters have shown clearly how all of this is an outcome of very natural processes.

And now we come to the realities and their specifics.

16

THE ENERGY CRISIS

Let's go back to Freedonia. But first note the following facts:

The U.S. trade deficit in 1972 was about $6 billion. In the year 1972 the United States had to import oil and gas to the extent of $6 billion. By this year, 1975, the cost of imported energy is expected to reach $15 to $20 billion.

And we are told that the balance of payments deficit must be cured. And the United States authorities are promising to cure it!

How will they cure it, and who is going to pay for $15 billion of purchases of foreign oil? Obviously the citizens of the United States will have to earn $15 billion more than they now earn from foreign trade to pay the bill. That means the United States will have to manufacture things pretty cheaply, and with an efficiency far beyond the present efficiency.

Now let's go back to Freedonia.

When we colonized the island of Freedonia we found a great supply of fresh water and several natural wells. Our prodigious industry, as we grew, required massive amounts of water. We used water—like water. We let the wells flow even when there was no one around to collect the water. We even let the water run into the ocean. We thought there would never be any end to the supply of water from those wells. Then one day a shepherd came from the far fields and said the well up there was running dry and there was hardly enough water for his sheep. So we said we will have to move the sheep to another pasture where the well is good.

One by one the wells began to run dry. And we woke up one day to find out that we were running into, of all things, a water crisis.

Our industry was faced with the prospect of cutting back, because our refiners could not run without a great deal of water, and our steam boilers required lots of water. Our people were used to using water—as if it were water.

Our leaders called a hurried council to decide what to do. All of the dowsers in Freedonia were called out to find new wells, but they could find amazingly few. Their report was that we had used up the best of the water supply, and while we would always find some new wells, there would not be nearly enough even to meet current demand, let alone the growing demand.

Our leaders were face to face with the grim fact that Freedonia would have to import water.

Now this meant using the productive efforts of men to build boats especially for water, and of manning these boats back and forth to a distant island, and of creating storage facilities for the water. It meant a steady stream of boats—so many that one water tanker would be unloading every 20 minutes day and night. Also, the islanders who supplied the water were going to charge us a fairly stiff price for their water.

Consider, for a moment, the amount of effort that we collectively must put into the business of bringing in water.

This is unproductive effort compared with our previous activities—just as our effort in the war was unproductive. We must divert the creative labor of a large segment of our population to provide our colony with water, whereas, before, this same amount of labor was able to contribute to our living standard—whether it was making wine to suit our taste or hammocks so we could spend our leisure time swinging in the sun.

Apart from the loss of this productive labor, we have to pay a bill for the water to the other islanders. We have to manufacture goods: shoes, pottery, or whatever; or we have to go out and grow more potatoes and corn (or else we have to eat less potatoes and corn ourselves) to send over to those islanders to pay for the water.

Either our living standard is going to come down, or we are going to have to work many more hours a day (not less), or we are going to have to come up with some very smart inventions to increase our productivity.

And that is the position of the United States in the energy crisis.

But the U.S. energy problem is complicated by a factor we did not have to consider in Freedonia. That factor is international money.

If the producers of raw materials—oil, nickel, coffee, etc.—see that the U.S. dollar constantly deteriorates, they will constantly demand higher and higher prices in advance. It may even be that they will demand gold unless the monetary situation is stabilized. To now they have been demanding higher and higher prices.

As this happens the cost of gasoline goes up; the cost of heating homes goes up; the cost of industry, which is almost entirely powered by oil and natural gas, goes up; and so all prices go up; and so we have an increased inflation. And there is a further erosion of confidence in our money.

Either inflation must be stopped or our suppliers are going to demand gold. If they do not demand gold outright, they will demand that the dollars they accept for the oil must be redeemable in gold when and if they present these dollars for redemption. This is the prospect that lies directly ahead.

Another method is to put an index on basic commodities and then, as this index goes up with the expected inflation, the oil price would go up accordingly. But this means that inflation would lose all purpose; it would be like a dog chasing its tail. That can only go on so long. Whenever the inflation stops—you have the deflation.

But some people claim this is scare talk. There is really plenty of energy in the United States. All we need to do is go out and develop it. Let's examine that point of view.

Is the energy shortage being exaggerated by the oil companies for their own purposes? Just how bad is this crisis? And what is the importance of energy in maintaining ourselves as a first-class power and having the world's highest living standard?

The cornerstone of man's existence on this earth is energy. It has been so from the beginning. First, a man had only his own energy. The most energetic could run the fastest and wield a club the hardest; and so he survived. The advance of civilization is the story of the increasing availability of energy through technology.

There were the lever, the wheel; and subsequently water power turned the wheel; and the combination of fire and water, which was steam.

There were coal, petroleum, natural gas, uranium. Advancing technology was able to harness and increase the efficiency of available energy: internal combustion, hydraulics, and the energy gathered from the force of water through the sophisticated use of electricity.

The United States became the world's strongest nation not without a great debt to her natural resources and the inventive ability that put them to use. The key to our power was cheap and abundant energy. Those days are over.

In July 1972 the air-conditioning drain in New York City proved to be too much for the available energy. There just wasn't enough electricity. Food began to spoil in freezers. Traffic lights quit working. A week of sustained heat would have caused a most critical situation.

Great attention should be paid promptly to such signals. Their message is tantamount to prophecy.

During World War II America was still so rich in energy that it could supply the fuel to drive all the navies and air forces of the Allies with some left over. By 1972 all the oil wells in Texas were producing full-out. U.S. flow was at 100-percent capacity. Imports for the year 1973 were almost seven million barrels a day. Without that oil U.S. industry would have been hamstrung.

By 1975 higher prices promised to cut consumption a million barrels a day. But this wasn't going to help the balance of payments very much because, at the same time, the fall of production within the continental United States, because of exhaustion, would sooner or later more than make up for the savings in consumption. The big import bill would have to continue, or millions would shiver in the winter and sweat in the summer.

Conservative estimates are that the United States will have to import 12 million barrels a day by 1980; and that the energy bill will be $10 billion a year in 1975; at least $20 billion by 1980, and $30 billion by 1985. That isn't taking into account any inflationary spiral that may develop in the meantime.

The flow of money for oil will be concentrated toward the Middle East, and the Arab countries are expected to take in $80 billion by 1975. By 1980 they will be collecting $30 billion each and every year.

This would make them the financial center of the world, with reserves almost equal to those of the rest of the world combined.

And there will be competition for this oil. The United States is expected to want 12 million barrels more each day; Europe 12 million barrels more; and Japan seven million barrels more.

Isn't there any way this energy can be produced in the United States, asks the average man—nuclear power, coal, somehow?

Facing the danger of dependence on foreign countries for two-thirds of energy requirements by 1985, surely there must be some solution.

It's all bad news.

COAL, they cry. Yes, the United States has enough coal for a hundred years, and plans are going ahead. But the president of the coal association says it will take ten years from the decision to make the pilot plants for deriving gas from coal to the time when the full-sized plants can make a substantial contribution.

Moreover, much of the coal is high-sulphur coal, and greatly increased use of coal under present technology would cause very serious environmental damage.

NUCLEAR POWER, they say—the breeder-reactor plants. Well, even working under the fastest conditions, and being optimistic about the technology, and allowing for the time lag to production, it will be 1982 before we have a big contribution from nuclear power. Nuclear energy is fraught with dangers of pollution, and no one so far has been able to figure out a way to prevent or safely dispose of the lethal waste of nuclear power. They guess they can handle it, but no one can assure us that they can.

SHALE OIL AND THE TAR SANDS OF CANADA? The Canadian Athabasca Sands are known to contain as much oil as all of the Middle East. Yet under the very swiftest of development they could not produce and transport a million barrels a day by 1980 and probably not more by 1985.

HYDROGEN—that's the ideal fuel. It won't be able to make its appearance on the energy scene in large quantity until the twenty-first century.

SOLAR ENERGY—Here, at last, would be a source of energy not finite; a nondepleting source that once established would go on practically indefinitely without the need for replacement or discovery, and **pollution free.**

Houston's Solar Energy Laboratory chief Hildebrandt has noted that solar energy would be competitive at present prices. The mirrors (silver-surfaced), once in place, would not need to be replaced. The silver mirrors would retain 80%-90% of their initial efficiency throughout the life of their use.

Very quietly, the Canadian government has been using solar energy in lighthouses on the Atlantic coast. J.N. Bellinger, a top Transport Department marine official, says the government will soon decide whether to switch to solar energy in numerous lighthouses. Its Prescott, Ontario, light station has been on solar energy for some time. "It's a good source that we are all going to come to one of these days," says Bellinger.

The fact that solar energy has been able to work at all in this low sunshine area, and that it is now under serious consideration for further lighthouses, ought to give a real boost to the use of solar energy throughout the desert and sunny areas of the United States, and the hot countries of Asia and Africa.

Here is the prediction of the Houston laboratory chief:

101

(1) There will be a 10,000-kwh. solar plant in operation in the U.S. by 1978.

(2) There will be numerous larger units in the 1980s.

(3) Solar energy may well provide 20% of U.S. energy needs by the year 2000.

Solar energy is one of the brighter hopes to replace petroleum. Unfortunately, it will not be of meaningful help for another 10 years.

PRUDHOE BAY IN ALASKA has a reserve of ten billion barrels and it has about 10 percent of the gas reserves of the United States, but Prudhoe Bay natural gas hasn't a chance of actually flowing into the furnaces before 1980. Chances with the oil are better, but the oil is being delayed by environmental considerations and isn't likely to be on the scene until at least 1977.

RUSSIA AND ALGERIA. There is much talk about liquefied natural gas from these two sources. Russian gas—if it ever comes—is also eight years away. There's no guarantee that, once the whole project is set up by huge American investment, the Russians wouldn't shut off the valve in case of dispute. Also that kind of gas would cost at least twice, if not three times, as much as the present natural gas.

Beyond 1980 there is a reasonably good chance that the United States can work back to self-sufficiency in energy. But an historic crisis will develop in the next five years.

In all of the world there simply is no alternative source to the Middle East. The United States has 38 billion barrels in reserve. Canada has 11 billion barrels. The Middle East has 300 billion barrels, and Saudi Arabia alone has half of that. This Middle East oil is already found, proven, and in the process of vigorous development.

Can't we use electricity? Well, electricity comes from water power or from plants operating on oil or coal. It is also wasteful of energy content, wasting two-thirds in the conversion from fossil fuel to electricity.

Seventy-five percent of all the energy consumed in the United States is from oil and natural gas. Industry uses almost one-third of all the energy in the United States. Transportation and utilities each use about one-quarter and private homes use 14 percent, leaving less than 5 percent for other smaller uses.

In the event of a serious energy shortage, industry would be hit first. That means a cutback in production and employment.

Making the energy picture worse is the fact that U.S. oil production has already peaked out and will now go into decline. As consumption rises by seven million barrels a day between now and 1980, production is expected to fall three or four million barrels a day.

Indeed, our land of Freedonia is in a bad way for well water.

What is more, the current costs of obtaining oil are disruptive to normal economic patterns of the industrial world.

The chief executive for the Continental Oil Company, John G. McLean, laid it on the line in January 1973. He said:

"Our growing purchases, coupled with those of Western Europe and Japan, will create major new centers of financial power. By 1985, the oil producing countries of Africa and the Middle East could be collecting oil revenues at an annual rate of almost fifty billion. Most of these countries are not yet ready to use new funds of this magnitude internally. And so large portions of the oil tax revenue will move into the money markets of the free world with impacts which are difficult to predict. One clear possibility is that these countries could become large equity holders in the financial institutions and industrial companies of the United States, Western Europe, and Japan."

Mr. McLean goes on to ask a most pertinent question: "In order to get the money to pay for this oil what shall we sell and to whom shall we sell it? We cannot look to the industrialized countries of Western Europe and Japan because they will be struggling to increase their own net exports to pay for growing fuel imports.

"Ultimately the situation can come to equilibrium worldwide only when the oil exporting countries are able to absorb greatly increased imports from us and from other oil importing countries.

"But they do not have the population, markets, and economic infra structures to accept large imports from us."

Mr. McLean appears to leave us without an answer. He points out that Russia will be the only major power self-sufficient in energy.

It is apparent that, in any military contest between the United States and Russia, Russia would immediately seize the Middle East oil fields. If there were to be a military contest for control of those fields, the Russians could blow them up—if the Arabs did not.

There probably is no greater threat to this world than the growing energy deficiency of the Western nations. The truth is that the Arabs have a world monopoly; even if we were willing to pay a much higher price, the commodity would not be available in sufficient quantity. The urgency of the truth is that the height of the energy crisis will develop before the end of this decade.

Historically, powerful nations never themselves suffered sharp deprivations by weaker nations simply as a matter of principle or out of respect for private property. Powerful nations have no notable reputations as good sports. Complicating the situation further is the competition among the powerful nations for the world's store of energy centered in the Arabian Peninsula. If one goes in to take the energy by force, will the others stand by? Will thief fall upon thief?

The Arabs are not altogether without their defenses. They may be likened to a blind Samson with his hands on the pillars supporting the palace. Arabs could mine oil wells, pipelines, installations of all kinds.

They could be prepared to blow up—like a hijacker on a plane—harbor installations and refineries. It is not conceivable that any large country could use military might to seize these energy supplies without the ensuing result of world conflict.

The situation will develop into one of three alternatives:

(a) Bargaining with the Arabs by various countries individually, and paying them off in hard, cold, redeemable money;

(b) Bargaining with the Arabs collectively by the Western nations, and paying them off in cold, hard money that they would then be willing to reinvest, because they would know that this money would hold its value;

(c) The introduction of armed force, where the world's strongest country will simply seize the energy—if there is any left when the smoke clears away.

The first alternative requires that the United States pay for the oil in warehouse receipts—hard money—gold or its equivalent. This will mean an enormous reduction in the living standard in the United States.

The second alternative is the most pleasant of the three, but may be the most unlikely. International cooperation is universally commendable, but rarely—when the chips are down—functional. Each country can find reasons why it ought to have a larger share. The Arabs—in view of their conflict with Israel—can find reasons why they ought to allot more of the energy to one power or another, depending on who is on their side against Israel.

If the third alternative should develop, the result would be so disastrous that there is no point even trying to imagine what we should do.

The reader may think that all of this is rather an alarmist reaction to the facts. Let me assure you there are numerous serious students of the situation who are no less concerned. Professor Nevil Brown, British professor and an international oil authority, prophetically warned a European-American conference in Amsterdam, in 1973, of the possibility of an Arab embargo of oil shipments because of the struggle with Israel. He said:

> . . . In the event of such an embargo the West may face the choice of capitulating or going in physically to get the oil.
>
> About the only other practical answer has come from Walter J. Levy, New York consultant to the U.S. government. Mr. Levy recommends an international agreement, virtually a worldwide rationing system of oil supplies. It would amount to a program of "equitably sharing import availabilities during an emergency." This would involve a program of stockpiling and a standing system of rationing.

If we look on the bright side of the situation we have to come up with the conclusion that the best solution is for the United States to pay for its oil in real, hard money. That is to say, it will have to reduce its living standard just as Freedonia had to reduce its living standard when it woke to discover that its wells had gone dry.

I must warn you here that a serious reduction of the United States living standard means a depression and the collapse of credit money. That can only result in widespread violence bordering on, or developing into, revolution.

This is the meaning of the energy crisis.

WHAT THIS MEANS TO YOU

It means you will find it increasingly expensive to drive your car. You will be faced with extra-large taxes for cars with motors beyond a certain horsepower. It means, therefore, that if you are at an average level of income, you will be able to drive less and your holidays will be confined to places nearer home. It is, therefore, wise to consider getting rid of your car with a big motor and buying a car that will take you twice as many miles comfortably with a small motor.

Remember that gasoline will be increasingly precious for years to come.

It means that at times there will be emergency shortages of both electricity and other forms of fuel and power. If you heat with fuel oil, it would be wise to install some storage tanks in your home to carry you over emergencies. Reduce your dependency upon electricity, because it is the most vulnerable, of all the forms of energy, both to sabotage and to interruptions as a result of shortages. Convert as much as possible to fuel oil; and arrange for the maximum possible storage. The fuel oil you have in storage will cost you no more, and it will not deteriorate. Check local ordinances first.

Do not buy a large home requiring a heavy drain of electricity or natural gas for heating or air conditioning. Watch all commitments concerned with energy and fuel, because these shortages are going to get worse and worse and worse. If you are buying a new home, seriously consider a small one, extremely well insulated. Avoid more space than you need.

Since power interruptions are to be expected you should have candles, of course, but, in addition, you should have either a Coleman gasoline light and a five-gallon container of high-test gasoline, or some kerosene lamps with extra globes and kerosene. Again, check local ordinances.

It might be wise also to have on hand a Coleman camp stove and a further supply of high-test gas. Shortages could occur without much notice in the event of violent social disturbances.

17

LAST DAYS OF DOLLAR IMPERIALISM

We have already spoken of dollar imperialism; but in view of the energy situation let's examine it briefly again. If the United States can print money and refuse to redeem it, and the recipient countries cannot use it at its face value in buying goods from other countries, then it follows that United States citizens are receiving oil, cocoa, steel, lumber, etc., at the expense of other people. By imposing a lower living standard on other countries, they are helping to support a nation that maintains a much higher living standard.

The Japanese worker in an auto plant who receives each week only one-third of the purchasing value of an American worker is not going to be very happy with his government when that government revalues the yen upward. It means that fewer Japanese cars can be sold abroad, and foreign-made cars from the United States are more easily available for rich Japanese to buy. So the jobs of the Japanese are being squeezed. If the upward revaluating process continues, as it is now doing under the system of floating exchange rates, it puts more and more of the weight of the high living standard of the United States onto Japan and our other trading partners.

When the U.S. Federal Reserve System printed bogus money, and this money found its way out into the domestic economy in the form of social benefits and subsidies, this money eventually became a part of the surplus that is spent abroad. With this money American corporations were able to buy foreign corporations. To the extent that this money was not redeemable back in the United States, they had obtained the foreign corporations for nothing.

Meanwhile Americans had been living high on the hog.

The subject here is probably the most difficult of all of this monetary discussion to understand. At the same time it is probably the basic reason why the current policies of the United States cannot continue to survive. The policy calls for others to give alms to the United States. *It calls for others voluntarily to sacrifice a part of their labor for the benefit of Americans.*

This is a deliberate policy on the part of the United States Government. That was obvious when the United States passed the unemployment law. The unemployment law says that regardless of the U.S. balance of payments abroad, internal conditions will be prosperous; employment will be full.

That is a very arrogant law.

The practice is exactly parallel to the case where you say, "I am the head of my household and my family, and my family is going to live as well as the Joneses or better; and that is my first consideration regardless of my balance of payments—regardless of whether I go into debt to others." Certainly if you go into debt far enough you can never pay them back, but that is a secondary consideration. It would be arrogant, and it would be foolish in your case, unless you were strong enough to enforce it on your neighbours.

All of the above is explanatory of the basic concept of this book, which is the Collapse of Inflation and its sequel—The Coming Deflation. All of the above means that when other countries refuse to go along with this any longer, the United States will have to pay its full way every year.

In the years 1971 and 1972 the United States had a total balance of payments deficit of $40 billion. In those two years alone it chalked up debts with the rest of the world equal almost to one-quarter of the total reserves of all the Central Banks in the world.

That $40 billion deficit represented goods and services and properties appropriated in other countries. Add to that $1 billion in 1973 and $10.6 billion in 1974. When do they get paid?

The American answer is this: The dollars are still good: you can buy American goods with them; you can buy American cars and washers and radios. We have no natural resources to sell you, but we have all kinds of manufactured products.

But the workers in the Volkswagen factory in Germany reply: "If we German people buy your cars, we have no jobs in the Volkswagen plant. Or if we are able to sell any Volkswagens to you we will have to work for lower wages to keep the price low. But already your workers in

General Motors get twice as much purchasing power for every hour worked as we do."

And so the German government is traitorous to its people if it continues to support and accept into its country this international counterfeit money that is used to buy the services of Germans, the goods of Germans, and even the corporations of Germany. (I use Germany only as an example.) *This is the fundamental position of the United States dollar throughout the world—as long as it remains officially unredeemable at the U.S. Treasury.*

This book contends that it is a law of human nature that one group of people will refuse to subsidize another group of people unless they are enslaved. And so this book concludes that dollar imperialism as described above is coming to an end. The corollary to that conclusion is that inflation will have to collapse, *unless it is strictly limited to internal inflation.*

If such limitation was practicable, a country could use an internal script that would not be acceptable abroad. But it is almost impossible to see how such money could be used practically unless the country were encircled with the most vicious type of foreign exchange controls.

Remember that whenever you take a dollar out of the country to buy some chocolate bars in Holland made by a Dutch candy maker, that dollar becomes a claim on your country. Even if it circulates to ten other countries first, there is always a last man on the end of the line who is going to send it back to your country and ask for value received. As an American you have received value in the chocolate bar, but somebody in the course of that chain letter is stuck if your treasury, ultimately, will not give anything for it.

If, ultimately, your treasury will not give anything for that dollar, then the Dutch candy maker who "sold" you that chocolate bar actually *gave* it to you. If he didn't give it to you, then the last man who ended up with that dollar for equivalent services rendered is the one who is finally stuck with the buck.

So, from 1971 to 1974, the United States obtained goods and services to the amount of $51 billion for which it does not agree, ultimately, to pay anything. All of the countries holding those dollars at the present time are hoping that some other country will take them in exchange for goods. But there are too many hopers and too few takers.

Today the United States is called the richest country in the world. It is like the man who lives in the big house on the hill and drives a Cadillac. He is called the richest man in the neighborhood, but if he owes a hundred thousand dollars more than he is worth, he is not as rich as you are, who live in a three-bedroom bungalow. And his collapse will surely come.

So there is no great mystery about international money and international balance of payments deficits. Money among countries on the international scene is the same as money among families within the national scene. If you go into debt you have to pay it. If you don't, then someone else has worked without compensation solely for your benefit. This was clear in the early days of Freedonia.

On the national scene, the manufacture of excess purchasing power by government is exactly the same as the manufacture of currency by counterfeiters. One is legal. The other isn't. But the results are identical.

On the international scene, the manufacture of money by one member who refuses to redeem his money is international counterfeiting. Collectively, the people of that country are enjoying the results of the manufacture of international counterfeit at the expense of all those who take it.

And that is how international money excesses strike at the living standard of all of the families within all of the nations.

When other countries refuse to endure this practice any longer, we shall have come to a very critical juncture in the way of life in the United States, and in the world. We are very close to that today.

Sooner or later dollar imperialism was bound to meet its Waterloo. It appears that the final confrontation between dollar imperialism and the rest of the world will take place on the energy scene and it will be triggered by the energy crisis. It will happen long before the end of this decade, and in fact is already under way.

In 1974 the Organization of Petroleum Exporting Countries quadrupled the price of oil. But after they did that the inflation continued so that, in February 1975, Kuwait was taking the position that it wanted to be paid either in German marks or Swiss francs; some of the other countries wanted a basket of currencies for a measure; and Iran wanted the price of oil tied to the index of inflation of commodities. This last would mean that the price of oil could not be forced down by further inflation of the American dollar—no matter how many dollars were printed.

This must represent the crystallization of the confrontation.

Indeed, it represents much more. It means that we have come to the end of the age of inflation. It means that we are coming off the drunk. The LSD trip is over. The illusions are disappearing.

It means back to earth!

WHAT THIS MEANS TO YOU

Prepare yourself for a reduced living standard. You are going to have to face it and you can do so more successfully if you are preconditioned.

110

It is really not so bad. It will mean more frugality; it will mean less waste. But there can be satisfaction in both of these. Happiness does not arise from waste, or extravagance, or even necessarily from expensive pastimes. Intellectually and emotionally happiness resides in oneself, but it must rest on a base of security.

Make yourself as secure as you can and prepare, if you have some soil, to grow what you can for your own needs in the way of vegetables, or, if you have a little more ground, by keeping a few chickens, or sheep, or a cow. You'll be surprised how much satisfaction you get from those home-grown vegetables, and how much better they taste, and how much more you enjoy your life by consuming the products of your own labor.

Your living standard is dropping, but that doesn't necessarily mean that your satisfactions are going to suffer. They may even be increased.

18

BACK TO EARTH

If raising the price of gold and making the dollar redeemable in gold is so essential to monetary stability, why does the United States resist it with might and main? Why not just go ahead and do it?

That question is widely asked.

The answer is: It would mean coming back down to earth.

Why doesn't the drunk who has been on a two-week binge and who has spent money until he is broke, and caroused until he is in trouble—why doesn't he voluntarily drink two or three quarts of coffee and come back to earth? The answer is the shock is too terrible to contemplate, and so he just takes another drink—and another—as long as he can get it.

The damage to the American position, created during an era of inflation begun 30 years ago, is so horrible; the overspending has been so great; the debts so huge; the bankruptcy so complete that going back to real money will be a shock that will shake the nation to the very roots of its social structure.

Why doesn't John Smith who lives in the mansion on the hill and drives the Cadillac, and who is in debt up to his eyebrows—why doesn't he quit borrowing money that he knows he will never pay back to his unfortunate creditors, and come right out and face the truth; and go back to work again? Because the truth is so terrible that he can't face it, and he goes on desperately hoping that somehow he will still come out of it. And he will go on taking money from people who may never be paid back, until he can get no more and he is in bankruptcy court.

That is why the United States virtually stopped the redeemability of the dollar by the Washington agreement of 1968, but continued to *pretend* that convertibility existed. That is why, as bankruptcy loomed, President Nixon formally closed the window on convertibility in August 1971. With a store of only $10 billion in gold, and even at that time with $60 or $70 billion against it, and with redeemability claims mounting like fury, the United States simply was *unable* to meet the claims. Had the United States paid out this last store of gold, it would have burned its last bridge behind it. Then even devaluation wouldn't have done any good.

If its creditors—the countries from whom it bought oil, cocoa, and lumber—ever refused to deliver on new orders, the United States would need gold; and if the United States had used up all its gold, it wouldn't be able even to get any oil—except on charity.

When Nixon closed the gold window it was not an act of considered policy. It was an unavoidable official notice of bankruptcy.

In 1973, with redeemability out of the question, the lack of confidence in the dollar grew so great that hordes of dollar holders wanted to change them into other currencies. That precipitated the crisis of February 15 that culminated in a two-and-a-half-week suspension of the money markets of the world in March.

Such a thing had not happened before in the history of world commerce.

The shock of the bankruptcy of the world's richest nation left the other countries stunned. There was no way they could foreclose. There was nothing to foreclose on. For the time being they continued in a trance. Their first groggy reaction was to stop paying the agreed price for U.S. funds coming into their countries. First a few, and then all, of the nations allowed the dollar to find its own value against their currencies; that is to say, floating (free market) exchange rates. But as the heretofore unbelievably U.S. deficits of $50 to $60 billion began to register in early 1975, the U.S. dollar broke to new lows in nearly all markets. The dollar fell so badly that, once again, Central Banks had to agree to go in and support it. (That is, to buy dollars with francs in Switzerland, with marks in Germany, with yen in Japan, etc. The dollar even fell against the bankrupt lira.) Other nations had to try to support the dollar, because the lower the dollar went the higher went the mark or the yen in comparison to dollars; the more expensive became the Volkswagen and the Toyota on the big American market; the more the sales would shrink; and the more unemployment would grow in Germany and Japan, already beginning to suffer recession. So it was with most countries of the world.

The floating exchange rates of 1973, which really represented a breakdown of the Bretton Woods agreement, proved to be slim protection for the other countries against the massive influx of the continuously created dollars of the United States.

A half-hearted effort, increasing the price of gold from $35 to $42 per ounce, hadn't helped one bit toward restoring confidence in the dollar. It meant that the U.S. gold stock increased from approximately $10 billion to $11 billion—a change of no consequence.

It is of vital importance to every person, whether he is an investor with a million dollars or an hourly worker at General Motors, to understand what will happen when the United States is required to pay its way as it goes.

If the dollar were to be made redeemable in gold at about ten times the $42 price of gold, the United States would have reserves of $110 billion. It is very doubtful that creditors then would bother to change their dollars for gold—just as the people in Freedonia did not care about asking for gold as long as they knew it was there, and could get it if they wanted to.

But the multiplication by ten would make a gold price of $420 an ounce. That would mean that the German Treasury with its $4.5 billion of gold would then have $45 billion in gold, plus the 30-odd billion in U.S. dollars it already holds, for a total in excess of $75 billion in reserves. Normal reserves, as I have said, until a few years ago were $7 billion. Such a tremendous inflationary landslide could imperil the strongest currency in the world. Such a global conflagration of inflation would threaten to destroy our civilization.

There is good reason to believe that the other countries, realizing that they have extended credit much too long, have discussed the funding of much of the U.S. debt. That is to say, they would agree to put off their claims for gold on a certain portion of the U.S. debt. I use the following figures as examples:

Assume the nations said to the United States: "You owe our Central Banks $100 billion. We shall set aside $50 billion of that for 20 years. In other words we will lend this to you for 20 years at only 2-percent interest. You will not be called upon to redeem this $50 billion for 20 years.

"However, to do that we shall require that you make your money redeemable from now on. We know you only have $11 billion in gold, and you still owe $50 billion over and above what we will fund. We will all of us make the gold price $180 per ounce. That will give you nearly $50 billion in gold, which is equivalent to the call we have on you for the next 20 years. It will make you fully solvent and in a position to redeem your dollars if you are asked.

"This will once more make the dollar as good as gold, and a hard and dependable currency. Stability will be returned to the monetary world, and we can all get on with our business of progress. In other words, you are back on your feet. But from now on we expect you to make good. From now on you must pay your own way as you go.

"What is more, you will have to earn enough surplus by the sale of your goods and the efforts of your people in the next 20 years to save up enough foreign exchange to pay off your bill of $50 billion that we have extended as your credit line. You won't be able to consume what you produce. You will have to produce $50 billion worth more than you consume in the next 20 years."

Here is where we get back to reality. Here is where the drunk must sober up. In the year 1972 the United States ran a balance of payments deficit (trade plus spending) with other nations of $10 billion. Again in 1974. If in the year 1976, then—on convertibility—the United States should run the same deficit, it would have to pay out of its gold stock $10 billion, reducing its total from $50 billion to $40 billion, and leaving it again suspect. That couldn't be allowed to happen. Consequently $10 billion less would have to be spent abroad. The cutbacks might be in the military (the international might), the monetary (international invest-ment), and in freedom (the right of a U.S. citizen to spend abroad).

While the American public slumbers—because it has been ill-in-formed by the press—this is the somber game being played out behind closed doors.

Convertibility would mean that the balance of payments must be in equilibrium. It would mean that if the United States spends money on troops in foreign lands, it would have to have a surplus in trade to meet that bill.

The redeemability of the American dollar would mean that the United States, like all other nations in the world, could not consume any more than its total population collectively produced. It would at last become a choice of guns or butter. Up to now it has not been a choice—it has been guns and butter both, even if the cost is borne by someone else absorbing bogus dollars. Under the new era of reality and of redeem-ability, U.S. industry would have to be more competitive. Which takes us back to the *real* wages paid to the workers in the various countries. In order not to suffer a trade deficit, U.S. cars or washers or dresses, or whatever, would have to sell at lower prices in order to get a share of the world market. That would mean U.S. workers would have to take less *real* money, and buy fewer cars, washers, and steaks for themselves.

Their take-home pay could only be maintained if the U.S. Govern-ment were willing to take less in taxes. Or a tax rebate.

The 1975 tax rebate of $16 to $20 billion was designed to keep the living standard where it was, and to allow the United States to continue to consume far more than it produced.

In common sense, it must be admitted that this tax rebate is a reduction from government income. A sane financier would say, "We've just got to cut down on expenses if we don't have the income. There is no other way. Either we must cut down on our airplanes and navies around the world, or we must reduce our social benefits at home."

But not the United States Government, and especially not the Democratic Congress. *They do not recognize natural law.* The defense budget must be kept where it is if the United States is to be strong. The social benefits must be increased because not as many people are working. The taxes must be reduced so that the economy can be stimulated.

Unless natural law is only a joke, it must be apparent that we are approaching a tremendous comeuppance; and that this comeuppance—when it occurs—will come home to roost on the hearth of every clerk and hairdresser in the land.

That comeuppance is really the "collapse of inflation" or, in other words, the "coming deflation."

The most dangerous aspect about the collapse of inflation is the probable unwillingness of American workers to take less pay, even though they already enjoy two and three times the living standard of comparable workers in other countries. U.S. workers do not know that the country has been on a binge. They do not understand that the enormous deficits are having a shattering effect on peoples of other countries, because the bogus dollars that are the deficit to a large extent are buying up goods and services in other lands, and these bogus dollars will never be redeemed.

They do not understand that there is a basic connection between their jobs and jobs in Japan, Germany, France, and elsewhere.

U.S. workers have not understood that it is a question of the collective population of each and every country consuming only what they themselves collectively produce, and that, if they consume more, other people in the world are the involuntary victims.

The likely result of such a program of harsh realism would be the collapse of labor unions, and if you care to project that into demonstrations and riots, you can arrive at your own conclusion about the results of the collapse of inflation.

If the workers, on the other hand, were to decide to take less and to put themselves more nearly on a par with workers in other countries, they would be able to *buy* less. So instead of two cars in the family, there would be one. The Japanese worker wonders why there should be two cars in the garage of his American counterpart while he rides a bicycle or a Honda.

But as soon as workers begin to buy fewer cars and fewer washers, and go to fewer restaurants, the jobs in the restaurants and in the automobile factories begin to shrink, and so unemployment begins to mount.

That is what began to happen in late 1974 and into 1975. And that should have been the tip-off that the era of inflation was ending. A long period of deflation was being ushered in.

Under the strain of unemployment a worker could not pay the installments on his automobile and his house. Remember, the upshot of this 30 years of inflation and credit has been the erection of a trembling structure of debt. The graph on page 67 shows the growth of public debt; private debt follows the same pattern.

When a worker could not pay his debts, foreclosures would result. The mortgage companies and the savings-and-loan-associations, who have lent out the savings of people to other people to build houses, would not be able to collect their monthly installments, and savings institutions would suffer a loss of confidence. The proposition is not very different for the banks.

Under such conditions the production of large industrial companies would shrink. We all know that profit appears in the topmost production figures: let's say the top 25 percent. With a quarter less volume there may be no profit at all. The result of this would be shrinking dividends— an outlook for much lower earnings. The result of that would be a nosedive in the prices of those companies' shares on the stock market. Then margins would be called right and left, which would produce air pockets in stock market prices, which would bring them down further.

The next step after all of this—unemployment and the need for money—would be the sale by the public of their mutual fund investments. But the mutual funds only have 5 percent in cash, and they would be forced to sell the stocks they hold. Buyers would be scarce and sellers plentiful, and more huge pockets would develop.

There is absolutely no question that, in the conditions arising from convertibility of the dollar, there would be bankruptcies across the land. There would be bankruptcies among huge corporations, which would reflect back on the banks that have lent them millions of dollars and hundreds of millions of dollars. Banks would go under.

People's savings would be uncollectible.

A fury of indignation, as unreasoning and as violent as the fury beneath the French Revolution, would sweep the country.

The only answer the government would have to such a situation would be a massive new printing of money, so that debt requirements and margins could be met. To anyone who has followed this book thus far, the meaning of that is abundantly clear. If someone owed you a thousand dollars, he would still pay you a thousand dollars, but in order to make this possible the government would have doubled, tripled, or quadrupled the money supply, and you would only realize $250 in purchasing power. So three-quarters of what you had lent the man would have been taken away from you. All creditors would find themselves suckers; all debtors would find themselves fully paid up, although only having paid, literally, a portion of the debt.

But for those who have followed this book, this is no remedy either. Not one crust of bread has been created by doubling the money supply. Not one market has been opened to one American automobile in other parts of the world. The only way that market can be opened—under dollar convertibility—is for the American nation to produce as cheaply as the other nations. It's a hard answer, but there isn't any other.

This was not always necessary, because America had a technology and an ingenuity far ahead of any other country in the world. Also it had the mass market to exploit this technology and ingenuity, and other countries did not. So it became the richest nation.

Today other countries also have similar technology. The Common Market also has a vast market area of more than 200 million people.

Dollar redeemability means coming back to reality. Coming back to reality means competing with all of the rest of the world. Competing means lower wages. Lower wages means the scenario above. That means repudiation, because there is nothing in the treasury or elsewhere to back this debt.

If anybody can show me a flaw in this logic, or a substitute form of logic, I would dearly love to see it. In seven years of study I am unable to discern any other scenario.

But that is not totally the end of the story. If this had happened 20 years ago it wouldn't have been nearly as bad—even five years ago, when it should have happened. Now the energy crisis has struck the United States. Now it will be necessary to pay *real* money to obtain energy to run factories. It is already evident, although it may not yet have come about, that the rest of the world is going to go on hard money. That is, money that is represented by goods and services, as in the land of Freedonia. There will be much competition for oil, since Japan and Europe will require huge increases. *Hard money* will buy the oil. Unless the United States can produce hard money it will not be able to get its supply—without a world war.

How then will the United States purchase oil, nickel, copper, cocoa? The purchase will have to be made with goods of equal value, or with gold, which is exchangeable into goods of equal value. It comes down to gold. If the United States could find an enormous quantity of gold within its boundaries, that would bolster the national treasury and could buy any product anywhere in the world at any time.

Lacking the gold, the United States must earn the equivalent in commodities by the sale of its manufactured products at a competitive price.

When we come to convertibility we have come eyeball to eyeball with reality. Coming back to earth is painful, but it is inevitable—because earth is real—and that is where we live. It is not a question of *if;* it's a question of *when there could still be some inflation.* It doesn't really matter. The end result is still clear.

WHAT THIS MEANS TO YOU

Primarily, it means: Don't be a lender. Don't take second mortgages. Don't even take first mortgages. Do take cash, and convert the cash into reality—or hold it in greenbacks or short-term U.S. treasuries so you can move quickly, when you see which way things are going.

The exception to this is ownership, or stock ownership, of natural resources—but only those natural resources that are not likely to fall under government control because of a declaration of emergency (as with energy).

At the head of the list of the metals will be gold and silver stocks.

The big thing to remember is that we are returning from Alice in Wonderland's rabbit hole and we are emerging into the bright daylight of reality. At first the tendency is to close your eyes. No one wants to face reality.

19

WAGE AND PRICE CONTROLS

In 1973, as confidence in the dollar nosedived around the world, the price of commodities began to rise. It took more dollars to import copper. The energy bill loomed large. The price of gasoline and, therefore, transportation and, therefore, of living was going up. The price of food was going up. Housewives went on strike because of the cost of meat. They forgot that the cost of maturing a critter is mainly due to the grain he eats. They hadn't noticed that the cost of grain had exploded as U.S. warehouses were emptied for huge shipments to Russia and China. Everyone was looking for a scapegoat.

There really was no scapegoat. The man producing chickens, pork, or beef had found that his costs were suddenly higher. The packer paid more for the critter. The butcher paid more for the carcass. The supermarket passed on the cost to the housewife.

The villain was far, far back along the line. The villain was inflation, and it was the age-old story. Prices of commodities were not rising nearly so much as the value of money was declining.

Always, when this happens, there is a clamor for wage and price controls. That's because people confuse price with value. Erroneously equating price with value, they believe that since the real value of a pound of beef has not gone up, the price should not have gone up. There must be a dirty profiteer somewhere.

But is there? Or is it just a question of the immutability of value? I made an analysis of this in the "Quiet Corner" of *Myers' Finance & Energy,* October 19, 1972:

Can value be controlled? *Value,* says the dictionary, is "a fair or proper equivalent in money or commodities." And what is the meaning of fair? Fair means impartial or unprejudiced.

So value is an impartial, unprejudiced, equivalent of goods or services.

But a control is "arbitrary exercise of authority."

Usually authority and impartiality are enemies. So to control a value is not only contradictory; it is impossible. A value cannot be controlled. *A VALUE IS.* You can *SAY* that a value is less or more, but true value remains proudly independent of pronouncement.

You can control a price. You can say I don't care what the value is—this is the *price.* You shall buy and sell at this price. But the moment you say it, you have destroyed the *price mechanism,* which is a function of *value.*

The price mechanism is a fundamental wheel in the uneconomic engine because it shows what is happening to *relative* values in the market place, and is a reflection of supply and demand—as well as a reflection of the value of money. Monkey with this mechanism and you are inviting a major *mechanical failure.*

Price controls *do not recognize* changes in value. Therefore every time a value changes, the inflexible price mechanism gets a little further out of line. A man will not sell at less than value unless he is forced to sell. A man will not buy at what he considers more than value at all.

Fundamentally inherent in price controls is a distortion of value—as values change. This means an inevitable dislocation of the economic process.

That's why although price controls appear to work in the beginning, the cure never lasts.

As each month passes, certain values inevitably change. These accumulating dislocations lead to black markets which skirt the price controls; so it is a hundred percent predictable that the longer the price controls remain in force, the greater the dislocations are; and the more shocking the adjustment when they are removed.

At that moment all inflationary forces previously suppressed break out. Because they were suppressed, their breakout is dramatic; not only is the economy brought back to where it would have been anyway at the same point in time, but it has been further harmed by the shock of the breakthrough.

There is no way that a wage and price control can stop inflation; because *value* cannot be controlled; and value always *bosses* price. The commodities taken in total are not changing in value. It is the *money* which is changing its value.

Thus an attempt to contest prices is an attempt to control value. But value as we have seen is beyond and immune to control, so any attempt to control prices is a futility to start with.

How did the relationship between money and value ever get so badly out of whack? In our state of Freedonia, where money was itself wealth because it was the equivalent of a warehouse receipt, there was no way that a dislocation between money and value could occur.

How then did this drastic divorce occur? It occurred because money was changed by the economic authorities into a gimmick.

The divorce of money and value is forcefully demonstrated by the Federal Reserve Note.

20

THE FEDERAL RESERVE

What is known about the Federal Reserve cannot be told in just one book, let alone one chapter. The amount of information available about this institution is staggering. But what is even more staggering is the curious lack of vital data—essential facts that remain shrouded in darkness even today, more than a half-century after the Federal Reserve's founding. With all the information available about the Reserve, it remains an unknown quantity. And that is the point of this chapter, for often the unknown is more important than the known.

So let's examine the realm of the unknown. We shall confine ourselves to fully documented and unassailable facts.

Here are the main shockers about the Federal Reserve, each of which will be substantiated in turn.

1. Although the Federal Reserve has virtually dictatorial powers over the money and credit of the U. S., and although it operates at the taxpayer's cost, *it has never been subject to a public audit.*

2. The U. S. government does not own the Federal Reserve.

3. The banks do not own the Federal Reserve.

4. No one has ever succeeded in identifying the ultimate owners of the Federal Reserve.

Dealing with the first statement above, I refer you to the 739-page book published by the U.S. Government Printing Office, Washington, 1975, entitled, *Audit of the Federal Reserve—Hearings Before the Subcommittee on Domestic Monetary Policy.*

Refer to page 147.

Chairman Patman: "Considering the importance of this agency (the Fed) to the Federal Government and the day-to-day lives of every citizen, it is amazing that so much controversy . . . is still existing about this simple suggestion that Government auditors should be able to get inside the Federal Reserve. . . .

"The portfolio of the Federal Open Market Committee contains almost $87 billion of Government securities. . . . The Federal Reserve draws between $5 and $6 billion annually in interest on these bonds. It is out of this huge slush fund that the Federal Reserve finances its operations without coming to the Congress for appropriations or appropriations review, despite the fact that the Constitution of the United States says; and I am quoting the Constitution of the United States:

'No money shall be drawn from the Treasury; but in consequence of appropriations made by law.' . . .

"For too long the Congress has been satisfied to accept the Federal Reserve's own idea of what should be known about the Federal Reserve. . . ."

It is well known that even the State Department and the Defense Department are subject to exhaustive audits by the General Accounting Office, despite the highly secret aspects of much of their operation.

Should you think that there are really no mysteries to be discovered, please refer to the *Congressional Record*—House, June 16, 1975. Herein Mr. Patman is given permission to extend his remarks. He inserts into the record a letter from a U.S. citizen, which you might have written had you been informed enough to ask the question (page H 5570):

Re. Federal Reserve Audit Bill,

Hon. Wright Patman,
House of Representatives,
Washington, D.C.

Chardon, Ohio,
June 13, 1975

Dear Mr. Patman: . . .

What right has the Federal Reserve Board to refuse to consent to an audit?

Who owns the bonds and other securities held by the Federal Reserve? Who reaps the enormous profits resulting from the vast operations of the Federal Reserve System?

I think it is high time that the Federal Reserve becomes accountable to Congress and to the public.

Will your Committee kindly consider this Audit Bill in the near future?

Thank you.
Respectfully,
Mrs. Marie Miller.

Mr. Patman then inserts his reply to Mrs. Miller, and it is a very interesting reply. It is quoted here in part:

House of Representatives,
Washington, D.C., June 16, 1975.

Dear Mrs. Miller: . . .

Certainly I agree with you that the Federal Reserve has no right to refuse to consent to an audit, but the Chairman of the Federal Reserve Board, Dr. Arthur Burns, has refused and has stopped the audit.

You ask who owns the bonds and other securities held by the Federal Reserve. You doubtless refer to the portfolio bonds accumulated by the Federal Reserve banks, amounting to $93 billion. These bonds have been paid for once with good American currency and should have been canceled, but the Federal Reserve did not cancel them when they were bought, and now as the interest becomes due, the interest is paid to the U.S. Treasury and when the bonds become due, they will be paid again although they have been paid for once.

So I agree with you—it is high time that the Federal Reserve becomes accountable to Congress and to the public. . .

Sincerely yours,
Wright Patman.

One wonders why such important news never reaches the ear of the public.

In 1959, Mr. Patman complained:

"Our exposes are scandalous and shocking but they are only printed in the daily Congressional Record which is read by few people . . ." (Page 219—*The Federal Reserve Bank*).

In all of the many thousands of newspaper and periodical articles I have read I have never yet come across a comprehensive report, or even an uncomprehensive report, of what is going on with the Federal Reserve. The CIA, yes. The FBI, yes. The SEC, yes. The Federal Reserve, no.

Take, for example, the following. I don't know why you wouldn't see this in *The Wall Street Journal*. I think it's very exciting, and terribly important. (Page 369 from the aforementioned 739-page book, *Audit of the Federal Reserve*, Chairman Patman is questioning Governor Mitchell of the Federal Reserve Board of Governors.)

Chairman Patman: "You know, every important agency of the U.S. Government . . . has been audited except the Federal Reserve.

"Now the Federal Reserve, of course, has been able to get around that. The Federal Reserve does not even have to obtain its funds through congressional appropriations.

"They thought about going to Congress for appropriations and they said, well, we do not want Congress to interrogate our people. We have to stay away from that. Then they thought they would get the banks to put up the money for the organization of the 12 Federal Reserve banks. But the banks would not do it because a large number of them were not for the Federal Reserve.

"And then they figured out a way—and I think it is very clever—to get around this provision in the Constitution. That is, to try to divert the money some way so it would not be in violation of the Constitution. So they devised this very clever way by which they had the power to manufacture money, to create money, just like commercial banks have, except the commercial banks do it on a reserve basis. The Federal Reserve can create money on no basis at all—just create the money.

"Now they have created $93.4 billion to buy Government bonds. They could do the same thing and buy the entire national debt right now, and get $35 billion a year interest, instead of $6 billion a year interest they are now receiving. They could do that; there is no question about it.

"So we have to get to these things as we learn about them. I believe . . . you said 'the auditors do not audit the Federal Open Market Committee.'"

Governor Mitchell: "External auditors. That is correct . . . The outside auditors do not."

Chairman Patman: "Do you not have them audited by the General Auditor?"

Governor Mitchell: "The New York operations of the desk are audited internally by the New York Bank, and they are also audited by Federal Reserve Board employees. But that is all. The private firm does not audit those accounts."

Chairman Patman: "The private firm does not audit them. . . . Now there are a few questions I just must ask you . . .

"How big is the System's Open Market Account? . . ."

Governor Mitchell: "It is in the order of $90 billion."

Chairman Patman: "And how is that used? Is that used by the System, by the 12 banks?"

Governor Mitchell: "Well, it is owned by the 12 banks, and the interest goes into our gross earnings. And, as I indicated $5.5 billion went back to the Treasury last year."

Chairman Patman: "Yes; but the Federal Reserve does the taxpayer a gross injustice because that money is spent by the Federal Reserve without ever really having to account for it to anyone.

"Furthermore, William MacChesney Martin, who was Chairman of the Federal Reserve Board longer than anybody else, said that the bonds held in the Federal Reserve had been paid for once. Well, if they were canceled, as they should have been when you paid your debts, you would not have this portfolio. If you need money you can create it on the books of the Federal Reserve without reserves of any kind. That is what is done now. So you do not need this $93 billion portfolio from which you are receiving over $6 billion a year in interest. That is a terrible thing; to pay debts and then continue to make the taxpayers pay $6 billion-a-year interest on those bonds after they have been paid for. That is awful.

"So when you talk about turning back into the Treasury, you are turning back money that you took away from taxpayers that you should not have taken in the first place."

Governor Mitchell: "I think, Mr. Chairman, that I would describe the operation this way. That when we buy a Government security, we pay for it with a check."

Chairman Patman: "In other words, created money."

Governor Mitchell "That is right."

You could read on for pages and pages. You can judge for yourself whether after two decades on the Banking Committee Patman knows what he is talking about. I would have to think he does. Be that as it may, my big question is this: *Why are 200 million American people so uninformed of this situation?*

The lack of reporting on the Federal Reserve—*and what we don't know* —is the most shocking thing I know about the Federal Reserve.

I have gone to great length on this first point, so that you will be certain that everything included in this chapter is authentic. Let's deal with the three other points in short order.

Most people believe the Federal Reserve is part of the government of the United States. It is not. It has nothing to do with the government. It is a central bank, like central banks in other countries. Its money power is absolute. And no one in government controls it.

This last point was brought out in *The Congressional Record* of August 1962. When Congressman Patman asked former Fed chairman Eccles, "Does the Federal Reserve have more power than the President and the Congress of the United States?, the chairman of the Fed replied:

"In matters of money and credit—yes."

The term "Federal," as we shall see, was deliberately selected to fool people into thinking that they, the people, somehow controlled the money managers.

The banks are commonly thought to own the Federal Reserve. It is even taught in college textbooks that the many banks together comprise the Federal Reserve. But when chairman of the Fed MacChesney Martin was asked (1956), "Do the banks own the Federal Reserve," his reply was "No".

Here is part of the exchange:

Chairman Patman: "All right. No. 2 is that the banks own the Federal Reserve Banking System, and it is run by the bankers; it is operated for their benefit. That is a fallacy, is it not?"

Mr. Martin: "That is a fallacy."

Chairman Patman: "That stock, or that word 'stock' is a misnomer, is it not?"

Mr. Martin: "If you are talking about stock in terms of proprietorship, ownership—yes. . . . You and I are in agreement that it is not proprietary interest."

Chairman Patman: "Yes. Therefore, this does not convey any proprietary interest at all, and the word 'stock' is a misnomer. It is not a correct word at all. It is just an involuntary assessment that has been made on the banks as long as they are members. Therefore, the statement that the banks own the Federal Reserve System is not a correct statement, is it?"

Mr. Martin: "The banks do not own the Federal Reserve System."

The facts are that the banks' so-called "stock" (a) carries no proprietary interest—is unlike any other stock in a corporation; (b) cannot be sold or pledged—so does not represent an ownership claim; (c) does not carry any voting rights.

Nobody knows who owns the Federal Reserve. Ownership identity has never been published or revealed.

How did the Federal Reserve come about? One most interesting version appeared in an issue of *Frank Leslie's Magazine,* 1916.

According to this feature article, several of this country's most powerful men, including Senator Nelson Aldrich, international banker Paul Warburg and representatives of the Rockefellers and many other financiers, met in 1910 on Jekyll Island, the private Georgia estate of J.P. Morgan.

For nine days, according to the article, these men worked out the "Aldrich Plan," which, with few modifications, finally became the Federal Reserve System.

Aldrich, a partner of the Rockefellers in the rubber and tobacco trusts, had headed up the national monetary commission whose job it was to tour Europe and learn about money—a subject we realized we knew very little about after the money panic of 1907 had resulted in a wide cry for monetary reform.

But the Aldrich Plan was initially doomed, because of the senator's connection with the powerful banking interests. Putting up Aldrich to recommend a safe system of monetary control was like appointing the fox to safeguard the chicken coop.

The attempt to sell the plan to Congress was made again—in 1913. This time the concept had a label calculated to assuage the fears of concerned legislators and voters.

Obviously it was necessary to avoid any hint of private interests or private banks or even the idea of a European-style central bank. What could be more democratic, more American, than the word "federal"? What could be safer than a "reserve"? And what could be fairer than a "system"?

So the Aldrich Plan for a Central Bank of the United States became the Federal Reserve System. A clever repackaging of the same old ingredients sold the scheme.

The Federal Reserve System issues federal reserve notes. When the government of the United States needs money over and above what it collects in taxes, it must borrow from the Federal Reserve. Where does the Federal Reserve get the money? It creates it out of nothing and charges the government interest to boot.

At one time, the Federal Reserve could only create money to the extent of our gold holdings. When the gold backing, first nationally, then internationally, was abolished, it was free to create without limit—and that is how it comes into our story as a feature player in "The Age of Inflation."

In our country of Freedonia the money was issued by the state. It all represented goods and service and it could be expanded according to the amount of goods and services. It was a money economy. Originally the U.S. economy was also a money economy. But when the Federal Reserve System was allowed to create money, then the debt was issued in the form of money, and it became a debt economy. Your assets were someone else's debt. Someone else's debt became your assets.

But the Federal Reserve System issued money on the credit of the United States, and all of the people of the United States were responsible for the payment of those debts. Remember, at the same time, that the people of the United States have no control over the Federal Reserve System.

The power of the Fed was not recognized by many. It is still not recognized by most. A few did recognize it. A prominent maverick banker, Leslie Shaw, stated then:

"When you have hooked the banks together, they can have the biggest political influence of anything in this country. . . ."

One of the most outspoken critics of the Federal Reserve, attorney Alfred Crozier of Cleveland, told the Senate Committee:

"The so-called administration currency bill grasps just what Wall Street and the big banks for twenty-five years have been striving for. That is private instead of public control of currency.

"This robs the government and the people of all effective control over the public's money, invests in the banks exclusively the dangerous power . . . It puts this power in one central bank."

Thomas Jefferson had said long ago: "A private central bank issuing the public currency is a greater menace to the liberties of the people than a standing army."

On December 17, 1913, five days before the Fed bill was enacted, Henry Cabot Lodge wrote:

"The bill as it stands seems to me to open the way to a vast inflation of currency . . . I do not like to think that any law can be passed which will make it possible to submerge the gold standard in a flood of irredeemable paper currency."

The statesman Elihu Root called the bill an outrage on our liberties and he prophetically said: "Long before we wake up from our dreams of prosperity through an inflated currency, our gold, which alone could have kept us from catastrophe, will have vanished and no rate of interest will tempt it to return."

Was he right? Only sixty years later, in the year 1973, no amount of interest was able to coax gold back to the United States. Money fleeing the United States would rather earn no interest at all in a stronger currency than to return into the form of dollars and risk further devaluation. The money hemorrhage abated in 1974, but began to reoccur in 1975. The dollar fell to historic lows on world exchanges.

The 60-year-old Fed had been sired by Messrs. Morgan, Aldrich, Warburg, et al. and delivered by President Wilson. The squalling voice of the child was muffled so the public wouldn't know that he was born.

Woodrow Wilson was a university professor. He knew about as much on the subject of money as any other university professor. His backers, however, knew what the people wanted and he was swept into office on a promise that he would give the people of the United States a law on money and credit that would be free from Wall Street influence. *Wilson was the candidate of monetary reform.*

And thus materialized the fear expressed in the prophecy of Abraham Lincoln shortly before he was assassinated:

I see in the near future a crisis approaching that unnerves me and causes me to tremble for the safety of my country; corporations have been enthroned, an era of corruption in High Places will follow, and the Money Power of the Country will endeavor to prolong its reign by working upon the prejudices of the People, until the wealth is aggregated in a few hands, and the Republic destroyed.

Wilson gained office on the promise to put through the "monetary reform" that he genuinely believed to be a *reform*. But within three years of the passage of the Federal Reserve Act, Wilson, too late, saw the light. He said:

A great industrial nation is controlled by its system of credit. Our system of credit is concentrated. The growth of the nation, therefore, and all our activities are in the hands of a few men . . . we have come to be one of the worst ruled, one of the most completely controlled and dominated governments in the civilized world—no longer a government by free opinion, no longer a government by conviction and the vote of the majority, but a government by the opinion and duress of small groups of dominant men.

In 60 years there have been no basic changes. The baby grew into a giant; the giant has become a Frankenstein monster; and the monster is inflation, whose hands now clutch the throat of Western civilization.

In the land of Freedonia the money was issued by the elected representatives in an amount equivalent to the goods and services for sale, or at least on their way to market. In the first instance they had no gold or silver.

Representative Wright Patman, among others, sincerely believes that gold and silver are unnecessary so long as the elected representatives are in charge of the money and credit. But we saw that even in Freedonia politicians soon realized that those who promised the most would be elected, and so the Promisers began, before long, to control the government—and therefore the money.

In *absolute terms* Mr. Patman is right. It is human nature that destroys Mr. Patman's theory. Only when man is bound and limited by a Scale—like the one that keeps the butcher honest—can he be restrained from his proclivity to aggrandize himself by means of subterfuge and methods that are not immediately discernible; that is to say—inflation.

Admittedly it is much better that Congress should create and control the money than that an agency of special interests should have this power—infinitely better. But it is better still if these representatives are forced to weigh the meat on a scale with the needle visible to the customer. Gold and silver are that scale.

There can be no honesty in government, no enduring republic, until the elected representatives of the people are in control of the money and the credit, and until they also are controlled by the discipline of exhaustible commodities beyond which they dare not go in the creation of the money and credit.

Here is what Chairman Patman of the House Committee on Banking and Currency sees for the future. Make your judgment about his soundness. He has to be considered one of the major monetary authorities in the U.S. (Page 177, *Audit of the Federal Reserve*).

"The Federal Reserve is allowed to manufacture money. It does not cost them a penny.

"I asked Dr. Burns a question in a hearing not so long ago before this subcommittee. I said, Mr. Chairman, who owns the title to the $70 billion of bonds (at that time) in the open market portfolio that have been purchased on credit initiative? Dr. Burns said the $70 billion (at that time) on the books of the Federal Reserve banks are owned by the Federal Reserve banks.

"Now that looks to me like that is a complete departure from our monetary system, if we are going to let the Federal Reserve own those bonds. . .

"I asked Dr. Burns, I said, who owns them, and he said the Federal Reserve banks own them, as distinguished from the Government. So I think it is a serious question here. If we let the Federal Reserve continue to do that, they will not only have squatters' rights, as we say in the West, on land titles, but a precedent set as to what they can do in the future.

"If they can take the money that they create without any reserves of any kind behind money and buy bonds that are interest bearing and do not cancel them when they are bought, why they have a privilege there that no other financial institution on Earth ever had, to my knowledge. A counterfeiter is fined heavily if he is caught doing what the Federal Reserve is doing. . . .

"If this is carried to its logical end, the Federal Reserve will not quit with just. . . its (present) portfolio. It has been increasing the portfolio by the billions every year in the last few years. They will go ahead and they will buy the entire national debt if they want to in exactly the same way. There would be no restriction against them doing it. *And then, after they own the entire national debt and get about $35 billion a year interest on it, none of which cost them anything, they will then commence to acquire private bonds or the bonds of States, counties, and cities and other political subdivisions. There will be nothing to stop them.*

"It looks to me like if we do not settle this question and settle it now, we are in for a lot of questions involving the solvency and security of this Nation.

"Would you like to comment on that?"

"Mr. Staats: Well, I do not believe I have any general comment to make, Mr. Chairman."

This chapter makes no pretense at being comprehensive regarding the Federal Reserve. But a book on money must include at least the *basic* naked truth. No book on money can be worth its salt unless you know at least this much about the Federal Reserve.

Without the control of the money in the hands of the elected representatives of the people, our country of Freedonia was transformed, like the United States, into a country subservient to monetary impostors.

21

A SWAP FOR A SWAP FOR A SWAP

The United States Treasury has admitted that Federal Reserve notes are not in themselves lawful money.

This may seem a strong statement but you can check it if you happen to have in your possession Federal Reserve notes of older vintage. You will see that until a few years ago they all carried this inscription:

"This note is legal tender for all debts, public and private, and is redeemable in lawful money at the United States Treasury, or at any Federal Reserve Bank."

This inscription appeared on all Federal Reserve notes. The one photographed below was signed by Henry H. Fowler in 1950.

The natural conclusion is that if this note is redeemable in lawful money, it certainly cannot in itself be lawful money.

The confrontation between the promise and its fulfillment is not without a touch of humor, as demonstrated by the correspondence between Mr. A. F. Davis and the U.S. Treasury herewith reproduced:

A. F. DAVIS
12818 Coit Road
Cleveland 1, Ohio

December 9, 1947

Honorable John W. Snyder,
Secretary of the Treasury,
Washington, D.C.

Dear Sir:

I am sending you herewith via Registered Mail one ten dollar Federal Reserve note.

On this note is inscribed the following: "This note is legal tender for all debts, public and private, and is redeemable in lawful money at the United States Treasury or at any Federal Reserve Bank."

In accordance with this statement, will you send to me $10.00 in lawful money.

Very truly yours,
(Signed) A. F. Davis

TREASURY DEPARTMENT
FISCAL SERVICE
Washington 25

December 11, 1947

Mr. A. F. Davis,
12818 Coit Road,
Cleveland 1, Ohio.

Dear Mr. Davis:

Receipt is acknowledged of your letter of December 9th with enclosure of one ten dollar ($10.) Federal Reserve Note.

In compliance with your request, two five dollar United States notes are transmitted herewith.

Very truly yours,
(Signed) M. E. Slindee, Acting Treasurer

A. F. DAVIS
12818 Coit Road
Cleveland 1, Ohio

December 23, 1947

Mr. M. E. Slindee,
Acting Treasurer,
Treasury Department,
Fiscal Service,
Washington 25, D.C.

Dear Sir:

Receipt is hereby acknowledged of two $5.00 United States notes, which we interpret from your letter are to be considered as lawful money.

Are we to infer from this that the Federal Reserve notes are not lawful money?

I am enclosing one of the $5.00 notes which you sent to me. I note that it states on the face, "The United States of America will pay to the bearer on demand five dollars."

I am hereby demanding five dollars.

Very truly yours,
(Signed) A. F. Davis

TREASURY DEPARTMENT
FISCAL SERVICE
Washington 25

December 29, 1947

Mr. A. F. Davis,
12818 Coit Road,
Cleveland 1, Ohio.

Dear Mr. Davis:

Receipt is acknowledged of your letter of December 23rd, transmitting one $5. United States Note with a demand for payment of five dollars.

You are advised that the term "lawful money" has not been defined in federal legislation. . .

The $5. United States note received with your letter of December 23rd is returned herewith.

Very truly yours,
(Signed) M. E. Slindee, Acting Treasurer

I wondered whether there might have been some change in the Treasury reaction to the redemption of its promise in the 23 years since 1947 when Mr. Davis wrote his letters; so on April 14, 1970, I wrote to Treasury Secretary David Kennedy as reproduced below:

April 14, 1970

Mr. David Kennedy,
Secretary of the Treasury,
U.S. Treasury Department,
Washington, D.C. USA

Dear Sir:

I am enclosing two $100 Federal Reserve notes inscribed . . . "Redeemable in lawful money at the United States Treasury, or at any Federal Reserve Bank", one signed by Henry Morgenthau, Jr. (1934); one signed by Henry H. Fowler (1950), both Secretaries of the Treasury.

Webster defines redeemable "to pay off (mortgage or note) . . ."—"to convert (paper money) into coin"—"to fulfill as a promise."

That is what I ask for here.

The reason I approach you directly is that Federal Reserve branches have in the past failed to make good on this pledge of the U.S. Treasury. Instead they have claimed that the note is in itself lawful money. This is unacceptable: *For to make a promise, and in the next breath to say that the promise is its own fulfillment is patently absurd.*

To maintain that the promise can be fulfilled by repetition of the promise (another Federal Reserve note) is likewise patently absurd. To point to subsequent legislation nullifying the promise (as Fed branches have done) is patently a repudiation of the promise.

I do not think that you will repudiate on the written pledge of a U.S. Secretary of the Treasury.

I confront you here with the solemn guarantee of the richest nation in the world, and I am asking that the promise be fulfilled. I do not know what you will send me as lawful money but you must know what the U.S. Treasurers called lawful money in 1934 and in 1950, when they wrote these promises. I do know you have silver dollars in the Treasury and I will be satisfied with them.

Thanking you in advance.

Yours very truly,
MYERS' FINANCE REVIEW
(Signed) C. V. Myers

P.S. Since I have several thousand dollars in these pledges, this is no academic exercise, but a matter of considerable material importance.

Here is the reply from the U.S. Treasury.

THE DEPARTMENT OF THE TREASURY
FISCAL SERVICE
Washington, D.C. 20220

May 12, 1970

Mr. C. V. Myers
Myers' Finance Review
903 Lancaster Building
Calgary 2, Alberta

Dear Mr. Myers:

Your letter of April 14, 1970, addressed to the Secretary, has been referred to me for reply.

As you have been informed, the two $100. Federal Reserve Notes which you forwarded with your letter are lawful money. United States notes and coin of the United States are also lawful money.

Silver dollars have not been issued since March 25, 1964, when the Secretary exercised the option granted him by section 2 of the Act of June 4, 1963 (31 U.S.C. 1964 ed., 405 a-1) and determined that silver certificates were thereafter exchangeable only for silver bullion. Prior to March 25, 1964, only the holders of silver certificates had an absolute right to exchange them for silver dollars.

Your two $100 Federal Reserve Notes are returned herewith.

Very truly yours,
(Signed) J. P. Purall
Special Assistant Treasurer

Enclosures: 2

My commentary then was, and remains, as follows:

The U.S. promise to redeem mountains of Federal Reserve notes in world Central Banks is worth no more than their discredited promise to me. How severely can we censure Kosygin when he said, in a different context (Cambodia):

"What is the value of international agreements, which the United States is or intends to be a party to, if it so unceremoniously violates its obligations?"

I say that the violation of a solemn understanding—whether it is related to a sovereign boundary, or a promissory note—proves a mentality of LAWLESSNESS. That the U.S. bureaucracy and executive branch—having trampled their Constitution—have raped all LAW—and that the lawlessness of the population did not begin at the bottom. It began long ago at the top— and *REMAINS ALIVE TODAY* at the TOP.

I couldn't know then how prophetic that commentary would be. It was not until August 1971 that President Nixon officially repudiated the claims of Foreign Central Banks for the lawful money of the United

States, which of course had always been convertible into gold. Nor did I have any idea of the upcoming disgrace in the highest echelons of the American government that was Watergate.

WHAT THIS MEANS TO YOU

The meaning to you as an individual, of course, is that in the Federal Reserve notes you have a promise from the United States Treasury. Today the promise is that if you take in a $10 Federal Reserve note they will give you ten United States dollars—in other words, another Federal Reserve note. And if you take in the second note they will exchange it for a third note. So the promise is redeemable by a promise to redeem a promise to redeem a promise to infinity. There is no end to the rainbow.

U.S. money is in itself worthless as far as the U.S. Treasury is concerned, and it is only useful to you when you buy something from John Doe if John Doe has the confidence that he can slough it off on Mike Smith, who will again slough it off on Bill Jones.

To you this means that as long as there is confidence the note is as good as money, but, if the confidence stops, the note is worth no more than the paper it is printed on.

So it is okay to hold greenbacks and *short-term* treasury bills as long as confidence remains, but you must be alert.

22

THE TRANSFORMATION

During 1973 the printing presses of the United States spewed forth such an addition to world money that in three years the world's Central Banks had accumulated reserves greater than the sum of all the past cumulative reserves of all the Central Banks in world history.

The Central Banks were trying desperately to keep the dollars locked in their treasuries. When the dollars came into Germany, for example, the German government had to issue German marks to absorb those dollars. In a few years, since 1968, Germany's reserves had risen from the normal figure of $7 billion to more than $30 billion. Japan's reserves have risen from $5 billion to more than $25 billion.

The recipient governments were frightened to death that all those marks in Germany and those yen in Japan would get into circulation and start a runaway inflation. They were between the devil and the deep blue sea. If they took in the dollars, they were risking the ruin of their currencies. If they refused to buy the dollars, it meant that the dollar depreciated against their currencies because huge offerings would not be taken up. When there is a greater supply than a demand in any marketplace, the price of the offering goes down. But if the dollar went at too big a discount, then these countries were at a terrible trade disadvantage with the United States. Their products would be high-priced in the United States and American Buicks would be low-priced in their own countries. This would mean unemployment in these other countries.

The unrestrained flow of American money and credit caused a growing resentment and mounting international complaints. The U.S. Treasury merely replied, "What are you going to do about it?"

In Europe this became known as dollar imperialism. But the question was a good one. What were they going to do about it?

There was an answer, but it was a most unappetizing answer. These countries could go on the gold standard, let the dollar depreciate—and erect trade barriers against the depreciating dollar. They knew, of course, that if they went on gold the dollar would go down drastically, not 10 percent, but maybe 20 percent or 40 percent. Who knew how far? If that happened they would have to erect tariff barriers of 20 percent or 40 percent, or whatever.

This would, of course, bring retaliation from the United States. A full-fledged trade war would be set in motion. This would precipitate a depression in every country in the world.

It was exactly such trade barriers that had caused the last depression and the resulting unemployment in all countries. There was no easy answer for any country. For five years they had been increasingly at the mercy of policies made in Washington—the money created by the Federal Reserve—and consequent dollar imperialism on a global basis.

The crises had become commonplace, and they had the habit of blowing up overnight. On February 12, 1973, the U.S. dollar, after three days of wild currency trading, was devalued by 10 percent. The money managers said that would cure it. Only two weeks later another currency tornado blew up and Germany was forced to absorb $2 billion in a single day. The exchanges of the world closed. They closed on the Wednesday of that week and they remained closed for the next two successive weeks. This was unheard of. Had it been prophesied a few years back, the experts would have said it could never happen.

After nearly three weeks of closure and countless high level meetings, finance ministers and the money managers simply disbanded—bankrupt of any solution at all. They merely said there was a great spirit of cooperation and they thought the crisis had been cured, at least temporarily.

President Nixon was making a show of keeping the U.S. budget at $257 billion. Even that figure meant a deficit of $12 billion. That would be $12 billion for which there were no goods and services. Unless it could be collected in taxes it would have to be manufactured by the Fed. Much of this money too would find its way into other Central Banks before the year was out.

Thus, in retrospect, the monetary troubles of 1973 can be seen, at least partially, as a consequence of a policy that started with the formation of the Federal Reserve in 1913. This policy had taken 60 years to reach its climax. Now it threatened the way of life not only of the American nation but of all the nations.

It was a problem far larger than anyone had ever dreamed. It was so monstrous that the authorities were reluctant even to verbalize it.

Throughout history there have been disastrous inflations, but they have involved usually only one country at a time. Now the inflation had reached into every corner of the planet. Unless a part of the world could suddenly stabilize itself, there would not be a safe island in the whole basin of the monetary flood. That kind of condition is an invitation to revolution, and perhaps simultaneous revolutions in several countries.

That is why it is valid to talk of the end of an era. Revolutions bring on a new way of life, and monetary revolutions are no exception.

We seldom realize what is happening until it is over. What is so clear in retrospect is hardly discernible while it is taking place. So it was not discernible to the American people or to any other people that a way of life was coming to an end. It was not even discernible to them that the inflation would get completely out of control before it was over. For, even in the fall of 1974, governments spoke boldly of the battle against inflation, while at the same time enjoying vigorous economic growth. The patient was sick unto death, but the doctors confidently toasted him to win the hundred-yard dash.

And all of this can be traced to the violation of the greatest document in the world outside of the Bible itself. That is the violation of the U.S. Constitution by the Federal Reserve Act of 1913.

Congress has no power whatsoever except the power given it by the Constitution. The Constitution is the *ultimate power*. It defines the powers of Congress and the limits of the congressional power. It outlines the rights of Congress. It specifically says that any rights not specifically given to Congress may not be assumed by Congress and must, if any such rights have been overlooked, go to the states.

The Federal Reserve Act is clearly unconstitutional on the grounds that Congress did not have the *right to delegate* its authority.

For instance, if you give your son the power of attorney over your interests while you are away on a long trip, does that give your son the right to delegate this power to a friend of his own choosing? What are involved here are *two* separate rights. One is the right to coin the money of the United States. The second is the right to delegate that authority. Congress has the first but not the second.

Later on, the Supreme Court, in a time of crisis, prostituted itself by agreeing that the Federal Reserve Act was constitutional because Congress thought it "necessary and proper."

The truth is that the Constitution was designed to restrain Congress, *regardless of what it thought.* The Constitution had provided that any unanimously desired alterations or additions could be effected by a constitutional amendment, requiring the assent of two-thirds of both houses and legislative assent by three-fourths of all the states. The Federal Reserve Act would have required a constitutional amendment to make it legal. There wasn't a chance such an amendment could ever get by the people.

So the Federal Reserve System was born in 1913, a constitutional bastard. From that date, the money of the United States and the economic liberty of the American people began to deteriorate.

The dollar, which was once backed 100 percent by gold, was later, under duress, reduced to 40-percent backing, later to 25-percent backing. Then, under Lyndon Johnson, all gold backing was removed from the domestic dollar. The gold backing remained under international claims. In 1971 Nixon repudiated even that gold backing.

The result was, of course, a continuing increase of money that was not represented anywhere by goods and services. That meant, inevitably, a deterioration of the purchasing power of the money. Every deterioration meant stealing from those who had saved.

When President Franklin Delano Roosevelt deprived the citizens of the United States of gold ownership in 1934, the last plank under the monetary independence of the American people was removed. It has taken 40 years for the house to collapse.

And now it has come to the point where the U.S. Constitution will be completely destroyed or the Federal Reserve will be destroyed. These two cannot coexist.

The first article of the U.S. Constitution, in Section 10, provides:

"No state shall ... make any thing but gold and silver coin a tender in payment of debts..."

That means that no state in the union can require you to accept anything but gold and silver coin as a payment for your services or materials. And most of the states reflect this portion of the U.S. Constitution, as does the Minnesota constitution, which says: "The legislature has no power to pass any law sanctioning in any manner directly or indirectly, suspending specie payments by any person, association, or corporation issuing bank notes of any description."

In plain language that means that no legislature of any state can pass a law that sanctions Federal Reserve notes.

An explosive case came out of Minnesota. There, a courageous Justice of the Peace ruled against the big banks and the total system of the Federal Reserve—and under trial by jury.

A Minnesota attorney, Jerome Daly, gave the bank a note for $14,000, secured by some real property. When Daly failed to make final payments, the bank foreclosed and bought the property at a sheriff's sale June 26, 1967. The bank then brought action under law for the possession of the property.

Daly claimed they couldn't take the property because they had given him *nothing* in the first place. In this very touchy case two justices disqualified themselves, so it went before a trial by jury under Justice Martin V. Mahoney at Credit River township, Scott County, Minnesota.

On December 7, 1968, the jury found both the note and the mortgage to be void for lack of lawful consideration given by the bank. The bank went for an appeal to the big court. Under the law it had to pay $2 to Justice Mahoney as an appeal fee. Mahoney refused to accept the two Federal Reserve notes because they could not be required, under the U.S. Constitution and the Minnesota Constitution, as payment. Justice Mahoney ruled:

> *Plaintiff's act of creating credit is not authorized by the Constitution and laws of the United States, is unconstitutional and void, and is not a lawful consideration in the eyes of the law to support anything or upon which any lawful rights can be built.*

The bank had admitted that it had created the money out of thin air. Mahoney declared: "The Federal Reserve notes are acquired through the use of unconstitutional statutes and fraud."

But now let us read the full text of Article I, Section 10:

> No state shall enter into any treaty, alliance, or confederation; grant letters of marque and reprisal; coin money; emit bills of credit; make any thing but gold and silver coin a tender in payment of debts; pass any bill of attainder, ex post facto law, or law impairing the obligation of contracts, or grant any title of nobility.

So you see, if Federal Reserve notes are legal, New York State can create nobility; The King of New York may marry the Crown Princess of Vermont. Texas can join Mexico; and Michigan can form an alliance with Canada.

For all of these conditions are a part of the same section of Article I of the U.S. Constitution.

The enforcement of Federal Reserve notes as legal tender smashes Article I in its entirety.

If Article I of the Constitution is smashed—no other article in the Constitution has any meaning.

Then there is no Supreme Court in the United States; there are no limits on the powers of the executive branch. In short there is no orderly government. *There is no law.*

That surely will be the end of an era.

And that is at this moment a reality. But it has not been realized yet.

145

The U.S. Constitution can only be restored by an amendment authorizing the Federal Reserve and all its notes, or abolition of the Fed and the recall of its notes.

The 60-year life of the Federal Reserve has marked the transformation of America into what has become, in fact, a lawless society.

WHAT THIS MEANS TO YOU

It means that regardless of any temporarily reassuring statistics, the crime rate will increase. As long as crime is increasing at the top levels of government, it can hardly be expected to decline among the lower ranks of the population.

It means that the very foundation of the Republic has been in jeopardy since 1913, when Congress gave away, without constitutional permission, the authority to coin the money of the country and to regulate its value. It means that sooner or later this confrontation between the Federal Reserve and the Constitution of the United States will have to come to a head. Either the Constitution will stand and the Fed will fall; or the reverse.

In any case, it will mean a monumental confrontation, a turmoil in the money of the realm. And it will place all paper and all promises in jeopardy. When this happens the metals gold and silver will for a time be the only reliable money. It means you ought to have both.

Until the control of money and credit is returned to the Congress, duly elected by the people, you will see continuing corruption in high places, the advance of lawlessness in government, and you may have to face a revolution where the issue will be settled once and for all. That is, the Constitution of the United States will survive in full—or it will be scrapped in full. You will go through many traumatic times before this issue is settled, and lawlessness will range across the land.

Be the protector of your own family. Be as far away from the great concentrations of population as you possibly can. The inflation that has resulted from the debt-money system used by the Federal Reserve will soon break. When it breaks, the results will come quickly. Inflation can go on for a long time. Deflation, when it comes, arrives like a precipitator in a solution. It is quick. You can take steps for inflation along the way. You have lots of time. In the case of deflation you must be ready beforehand.

The crisis of deflation can, within months, trigger massive riots in the big population centers. These are coming. Be the protector of your family. It is up to every man to use his own devices to execute protective measures according to the personal conditions under which he lives.

23

CREDIT VERSUS DEBT— THRIFT VERSUS SLOTH

The early land of Freedonia had a credit economy. People accumulated credit by producing goods and services, and they either held this credit in their own possession or deposited it in banks. It was perfectly sound to lend out this saved money at interest to others who wished to expand, and to accept real property as security.

This was the era of true progress. People spent after they had earned, or borrowed against what actually existed. They borrowed to produce. This production continued to expand the solid foundation of progress.

With the advent of the Federal Reserve and the evolution of totally fiat money (unbacked currency and credit), the life-style of any nation— Freedonia or America—undergoes a dramatic change. The change penetrates the deepest recesses of the moral structure.

People are encouraged to use now and earn later. To buy luxuries now for which they will pay at a later date. At a later date they buy more luxuries for which they will pay at a still later date. And so on forever.

The government initiates programs by borrowing money (bonds) for which it will pay at a later date. But when the later date comes, it borrows more money for which it will pay at a later date.

All of this creates an atmosphere of unrealistic euphoria. If you can have it, why not take it now and pay for it when you are dead, or let your descendants pay? The future is mortgaged to the present, and when the future becomes the present the next future is mortgaged to that. That is how it happens that the public debt of the United States is $450 billion.

The interest portion of Mr. Nixon's budget in 1973 amounted to nearly 10 percent of his total $257-billion budget. By 1975, the interest portion of Mr. Ford's budget was over $30 billion. Each year the interest grows on compound interest. It is easy for the most simple man to see that, in time, this compounding becomes a cancer of such size that it will involve the whole body politic, and like a cancer will kill it. The collapse of inflation is the kill.

The debt economy has another adverse, and more subtle, influence on the population. With everything so easy, it tends to produce a permissiveness, and with that decadence of moral fibre. Thrift becomes foolish. Why should any sensible man save when he knows that his savings will be depreciated, when he knows he can get more goods by spending his money today than by spending it tomorrow? Why shouldn't *everyone* borrow when he knows that what he borrows from his future will buy more goods today than it will buy when the future arrives? So debt mounts on debt. And moral decay sets in when, although a man knows that those who lend to him will be penalized for his benefit, he nevertheless condones the practice with the comforting thought that this lender will probably borrow even more from someone else, to protect himself; and so on.

For several years inflation was actually encouraged and welcomed by the population. Those on fixed incomes were suffering: their substance was being taken from them and given to the spendthrifts. In such a society it was foolish to be moral.

It is a small step from the immorality of accepting the property of others stolen by the government—to stealing the property yourself. The crime rate in the United States is not unrelated to the credit and money structure growing from the cancerous roots of the Federal Reserve's system of debt economy.

Also, under this system, spending is encouraged. Consumption is encouraged. Therefore waste is encouraged. Manufacturers purposefully design their products to become quickly obsolescent. The junk piles of North America overflow with steel, tin, and rubber from obsolescent washing machines, clothes dryers, television sets, automobiles, etc. With respect to the subject of waste, I wish to reproduce here a piece from the "Quiet Corner" of *Myers' Finance & Energy*, October 8, 1970:

CUPS OF COPENHAGEN

It seems to be predestined that the pattern for the masses is always to be designed by the few.

Probably no group with greater power over the masses ever assembled in one place than at the recent IMF meeting in Copenhagen. Perhaps some two hundred persons out of the three thousand could be considered the POWER BODY. These people controlling the finance ministries, and the Central Banks of the Western world, are molding policy—whether they realize it or not—which will set the pattern of the lives of hundreds of millions. They control the machinery that sets the limits within which millions will shape the pattern of their existence. The enormity of this concept when it struck me quite by chance—was shocking.

What was the objective of these men?

Clearly it was this: To maintain the status quo, to maintain the affluence; to prevent recession; to keep things moving; to project into the future what we have; *more of the same.*

At the Bella Centre there was a free coffee bar. I used it a lot. Every time I got a cup of coffee, they took out a sparkling new, clean plastic cup. Every time I set one down, they threw it in the garbage. They threw away thousands upon thousands of these cups. They gathered them up and presumably took them to some dump to burn.

And I thought: This is the affluent society—this is what we are striving to preserve. PLANNED WASTE. Surely the wanton dissipation of the fruits of our earth must be a sin.

Think of the search for these raw materials, the production, the manufacture, the design, the machines involved, the packaging, the journey to market. The cup is used for a single fill and the resources of our earth are tossed away. But we are not satisfied with that. No, we now must set these resources to the torch, using them to destroy the environment which supports us.

Those cups were good cups. Believe me. During the depression I know my family would have been mighty glad of those cups. I believe Asians would be glad of those cups. The peasants of China and India. But there is no profit in that. The manufacturers wish to keep on making the cups. Producers of plastic wish to keep on producing more plastic, so that there can be jobs and profits, paper profits of course. So the cups must be constantly destroyed, so that new cups may be made.

It's a tiny example. Projected, a nylon stocking is worn five minutes and catches a run. Both stockings go up in smoke. Think of the work. The fine material. Millions of pairs of nylon stockings every day—into smoke. It is not enough to have one car. Our affluence demands two or three cars. These, too, are planned for waste. The tin and the steel, the generators, the rubber, the enormous effort—the treasure of the good earth—they are all soon relegated to the junk heap, so that auto companies can make more autos, because we better not have a recession.

You find a little wear on the corner of your rug, and you throw it away. You don't cut it down to make it do for another room. You throw it away and the smoke circles into the blue sky. We must not have a recession. We must make more rugs.

The bankers better not let anything happen, because the politicians would lose their jobs if people couldn't throw their plastic cups away, and burn their stockings.

Tell me, where is the joy in this: *This mad rush to consume as fast as possible all the fruits of our planet and destroy them in order to poison the air we breathe?* Indeed, has not the whole world become infected with a strange insanity?

The U.S. is fighting might and main to avoid any hint of a recession. The Federal Reserve dares not allow the credit to be tightened. Otherwise, people could not burn stockings every day, could not toss used Mixmasters into the dump; they would be stuck with these wonderful products until they were worn out. But how could the manufacturers keep busy if people refused enslavement to fashion and waste?

More steel and rubber goes to the dumps, more unmended socks into the ashcan, while the wife drinks gin or watches TV. The chemicals that produce these products lay spoil to our sparkling rivers. The rivers reach out into our oceans until they lay waste to the habitat of the fish of our earth.

Now clothing manufacturers press hard on us to junk hundreds of *millions* of mini-skirts so they can make hundreds of millions of midis, also later to go up in smoke for something new. Wide neckties replace narrow neckties, so people will burn their old neckties.

And one thousand bankers who shape the economic lives of the millions struggle in Copenhagen to assure that this "prosperity" will go on.

Apparently only a deep worldwide depression can bring us to our senses. What else?

The era of inflation produced the era of debt, and the era of debt produced the era of waste. And waste, most surely, in this finite world of ours, is immoral, and thus has the moral fibre weakened.

With respect to the philosophy of credit and the era of credit, I reproduce a "Quiet Corner" from *Myers' Finance & Energy* of May 5, 1967, when the U.S. Government and the Treasury were taking all substance out from behind the money—both silver and gold.

ONE ACT PLAY
NOTHING IS BETTER THAN SOMETHING

Act I: Scene I
Hubert Humphrey enters the President's office.

LBJ: Hubert, Ah'm gettin' downright worried. Sit down. People have stopped borrowing. We've made lots of new money for them—but they don't seem to want to borrow. WORSE, they won't even spend what they're getting. This could ruin us.

Humphrey: (surprised) I didn't know that was bad. Don't you remember what they used to tell us about the grasshopper and the ant?

LBJ: Humphrey, don't give me that old-fashioned guff. That went out with the depression. Don't you realize that today you gotta keep on spendin'? If they'll only borrow—they'll buy. They won't own the stuff—but they'll buy! That makes a big Gross National Product. (Borrowing is at an alarming four-year low.)

Humphrey: But the more a fellow owes, the poorer he is.

LBJ: That is not true anymore. It used to be true, but today here is how it works: We throw a billion dollars into the bank. People borrow that and buy cars. So auto production goes up—stock market goes up. People who have stocks are now richer than they were. They can borrow more on their stocks and buy TV sets. TV stocks go up—and so on. Value on the New York board increases by billions of dollars. Think of the security that represents for further credit. So now everybody can borrow more and spend more. That's what I mean by stimulating the economy.

Humphrey: I'm beginning to see it now. Yes, I see it. The more we owe the richer we are.

LBJ: Exactly.

Humphrey: And so logically—the less a person owns the better off he is.

LBJ: Now you're talking. Follow that on and you'll see that "Nothing is better than something."

Humphrey: Hard to believe—but it does follow.

LBJ: 'Course it follows. Now listen to this. When people borrow more and own less they pay more interest—Savings and Loan shares advance—their profits go up. The whole economy starts earning more. When they earn more we get more in taxes. Then we start to give it to the poor—NOW EVEN THE POOR START TO BUY! Away we go again, and the market goes up some more.

Humphrey: Absolutely amazing—you're a genius!

LBJ: (smiling) My natural modesty won't let me take all the credit. I got good advisers—there's Gardner Ackley. You take Gardner—his economic forecasts are better than if I wrote them myself. 'Course—they're never right. But then, who looks at a forecast a year after it's been made? Meantime, it's stimulatin'—CRITICAL TIME FOR FORECASTS IS RIGHT WHEN YOU MAKE THEM.

Humphrey: One question—if we spend all that money—what happens when we have to pay it back?

LBJ: You're still acting stupid—you sound, I swear, just like an old-fashioned Republican. When you pay back you just borrow to pay back—MEANTIME THE DOLLAR IS ALWAYS WORTH LESS so when you pay back you pay back much less than you borrowed at first. With this easy money policy, when you borrow a lot you MAKE on the deal—besides all that stimulation.

Humphrey: (laughing) Those old-fashioned Republicans! I'll bet Henry Fowler helped you with that.

LBJ: Now there is a genius! He has just added a brand-new concept to our "New Economics." Want to hear it?

Humphrey: I don't know if I can take the shock of another concept.

LBJ: This one's a ringer. You know how it used to be when the creditors had all the power and the debtor was a "nobody." Why, they'd even foreclose on people. That's all changed now. We got her reversed.

Humphrey: You mean the fellow that owes money is coming to the top now? You don't say!

LBJ: I guess we do say! You see, all those countries that collected our dollars we been makin' over here—started to get mean and wanted us to redeem them with gold. Well, we did that for a long time—until we didn't have much gold left. When they started to holler—Henry lowered the boom. He told 'em right out. "You guys stop asking for gold or we won't pay any of you—NOTHIN!"

Humphrey: Don't we have to pay?—Won't we go bankrupt?

LBJ: (smiling) *THEY* go bankrupt. You see they have figured those dollars like pure gold in their vaults. If we say we won't pay gold then they got nothin'—THEY'RE BANKRUPT!

Humphrey: I get you, Chief, In the "New Economics" the debtor calls the tune and the creditors dance.

LBJ: You're on the beam.

Humphrey: But is it really true that paper dollars are better than gold?

LBJ: Certainly it's true! You take Canada. They've got quite a lot of gold up there, and we pay them thirty-five of our paper dollars for an ounce. Did you know that they pay an extra five dollars up there to the miners just to get that gold. That gold is costing them forty dollars an ounce but they're turning it over in exchange for our paper dollars. They figure that our paper dollars are worth a five dollar premium over gold per ounce. Does that answer your question?

Humphrey: Sure does. If they're going to pay us a premium for our paper dollars—then paper is better than gold! (Shaking his head) But those danged Europeans can't see it.

LBJ: But did you tell 'em—forcefully?

Humphrey: Everytime I said it, they threw another tomato!

LBJ: You got to use oratory.

Humphrey: Pretty hard to make a convincing speech when you have to keep dodging all the time.

LBJ: (rubbing his chin) We gotta make 'em believe it. Our whole "New Economics" depends on them believin' it.

Humphrey: Well I'm sure sold. I'm going to call Muriel now and tell her to go shopping and spend everything we got. Then tomorrow I'm going to borrow all they will lend me. I'll set an example!

LBJ: That's the road to prosperity!

Humphrey: (rises to leave—pauses at door) But suppose it backfires somehow —and it doesn't work?

LBJ: Ah dislike that question. Anything ah hate is a defeatist. (Pressing button) Ah'm just orderin' another billion dollars. Get outta here!

Humphrey: Yes, Chief. (Exits)

Scene Two
(Small classroom. Teacher has just finished reading play aloud.)

Teacher: Now children, I want you to study this play carefully to see if you can discover the revolutionary new truths developed by our country in pursuit of "THE NEW ECONOMICS."

Children: (snapping fingers excitedly) We already see! We already see!

Teacher: Here is a little true or false test. Read each statement carefully and write after it "true" or "false":
Nothing is better than Something –
Paper is better than Gold –
The More you owe the Richer you are –
Debts are better than Credit –
Spending is better than Saving –
Bigger the Debt, Greater the Wealth –
Debtors foreclose on Creditors –
(Children quickly begin filling in answers, and bring them to the desk.)

Teacher: But, children. You have put a "FALSE" after each of these statements. I don't understand.

1st Child: We discovered a deeper truth.

2nd Child: The deeper truth is: "False is True."

3rd Child: You see, if we had written "TRUE" after the statements, that would have meant they were FALSE.

Teacher: That's absolutely brilliant—and it is true—no, I-I mean false—No, true—No—I don't know what I mean.

Children: (chanting and dancing in a circle) False-is-true-and-true-is-false—true-is-false-and-false-is-true!

Teacher: Remarkable. You have qualified for the "NEW ECONOMICS." You will all grow up to be government advisors! (Exits.)

Indeed we have lived through an era of inflation and of insanity. We are now reaching the climax. In its final stages it will grow as the square of the square of the square. If some courageous government should come to power and step in, the cost will be deflation, a massive depression, and that itself will bring a revolution or near revolution.

So the collapse of inflation will mean the end of this era of our generation. People of 45 or under will find themselves in a world they cannot understand.

This era of inflation had its beginning when it was conceived in 1913, passed through its childhood in the next 20 years, went into maturity until 1965, and into decadence and old age in the last five years.

The era is finished.

24

GOLD AND THE PHANTOM

Gold is said to have a certain mystique. Bankers and economists use the word condescendingly. The inference is that only fools or, at least, irrational people value gold as money, but, if they don't know any better, what can be done about it? The uneducated peasants are, as a matter of fact, according to bankers, largely responsible for the world monetary dilemma because of their silly attraction to gold. If only the general public could have studied economics at Harvard, the world monetary system could run smoothly and this barbarism—an echo from the uncivilized past—could be put away forever.

Yes, gold rises from the uncivilized past. But we find that, as civilization progressed, gold became even more elevated as it came to represent the condensation of wealth. An ounce of gold, less than half the size of a small wafer, could be hidden away, and when the owner was ready he could exchange it for more than a ton of grain, which would be enough to feed him and his family for more than a year.

Moreover, it never lacked a market. It has never yet been rejected as money. No one can, by edict, destroy it, nor can it be tarnished by chemical or time.

Certainly gold has a mystique. Those who would denigrate it in the hopes that men or groups of men or nations would lose their desire to possess it—such people must be totally ignorant of human nature. For gold represents the ultimate security; and security is the foremost and most powerful motive of animal life on this earth—from the gopher to the king. And it represents something more—as old as the relationship between man and woman. I described it in a *Myers' Finance & Energy* article of August 1968, entitled *Gold and women:*

Since earliest history the two most potent forces motivating man have been gold and women. Eliminating one of these as a prime force of life is as unthinkable as eliminating the other. As a matter of fact, they are inextricably interwoven, and actually gold is part and parcel of the drive supplied by women.

To get a true view of gold, we have to go back a very long way. The U.S. may talk about demonetizing gold, but gold became money long before anyone thought of monetizing it. Only when we find out why can we assess the prospects for demonetization.

It is an axiom that behind most great men there has been a great woman. Behind some men there have been many. It doesn't matter. What does matter is that man has aspired to his highest potential because of a desire to please and to earn the affection and respect of women. The rewards of such efforts have usually resulted in material possessions, or in power through military might which led to material possessions.

After a long, long time these possessions came to be measured by a substance that was known as gold. This substance had absolutely no utilitarian value. It was extremely scarce, and it was extremely beautiful. To acquire any quantity of it demanded high spirits, enormous energy, imagination, determination, courage, and all of the attributes that we assign to greatness in men. And throughout all societies certain types of women were prized above others. And to get the most highly prized type of woman, one had to compete with the most able, determined, and courageous men. At first it was physical force. Later brain power entered the picture, adding leverage to physical force, so that a combination of brain power and physical force was able to triumph over mere physical power.

Now these men, whether they acquired more caves, more hides, or killed more enemies, rose above their fellows in the eyes of the most desirable women. Eventually their success came to be measured quite incidentally in terms of gold.

But where lay the power of this gold? Of what earthly use was it? It had only one use; it was adored by women. A man might lose his blood for gold. He might expire on the desert for gold. But if he was successful and he returned, and he brought as a gift this gold, he offered not only the gold but the symbol of his very existence. So gold was the homage of love. As such, nothing in the world had higher value—though from a practical point of view it had none.

Because gold was so highly prized by men, and because it was so scarce, a very tiny amount of it could be used to represent a large amount of material possessions. And it finally came to be universally recognized that nothing was more valuable than gold. So anyone would trade you anything for gold, when they might not trade for something else. Gold would buy what they wanted. It was the MAGIC medium. Unit values developed and it became the ultimate money. No Government had monetized it.

Once it became the ultimate money its desirability increased even more. It then commenced to represent the objectives of the acquisitive, the greedy, the power-hungry, the vengeful, the philanthropic. Even churches wanted gold. Its base, however, still lay in its desirability, its beauty, and its MEANING for women.

The meaning of a gift of gold was a confirmation of love and the meaning of its acceptance was reciprocal confirmation. Doubt it? Try it. Offer a woman of friendly persuasion a gift of a gown or a portrait, and she may appreciatively accept it. Offer the same woman a gift of gold of the same value, she will immediately tense up and reject it. Because it is an unwritten and completely universal law, that the gold carries a meaning peculiar to itself.

When the gold is offered it portrays respect, desire, and affection. If the woman cannot return this she will reject or resist the gift of gold. If she can return it she will be visibly touched, and sometimes overcome. When she wears it she will be radiant, not because of the value of the gold but because of the MEANING of the gold. And the gold wedding ring has been the universal symbol of love for thousands of years, graciously accepted by all women from barmaids to queens; and eagerly offered by all men from peons to kings.

Today gold has lost none of this romantic lustre. The demand for it has enormously increased, firstly because the population has increased, and secondly because of the emergence of a great industrial value for gold.

Because of this element called gold, men have perpetrated the most dastardly crimes, risen to the most heroic heights—gold has led them to the ultimate extremities of all their emotions; hate, love, fear. So men will accept token money as long as they KNOW it is as good as gold; but once they doubt that, they will not accept it any more. For when it is not backed by gold, it is backed by NOTHING.

Thus I bring you to this conclusion: Gold will never be effectively demonetized by edicts or by legislation, the Central Bankers of all the world notwithstanding.

The link between gold and silver is an emotional link. What may be said of one may be said of the other. Substitute the word silver throughout the above, and you will arrive at a meaning that will exist long after these words have faded; long after your most distant descendants have descended.

These are the precious metals of exchange that have existed throughout the long civilized history of man, and never in all that long history have these metals betrayed the trust that was placed in them. Yet the paper plasterers of today would have you give them up for some of the politicians' promises written with ink on flimsy paper, with a record of debasement and repudiation that goes back to Genghis Khan and his fiat money made from the bark of the mulberry tree.

These men are so uninformed about the history of their species and so blown up with their own importance that they believe a new-fangled idea less than 30 years in its current vogue can cancel out the track record of true money since the days of the Pharaohs.

They would banish gold, and what would they use to chase it away with? A phantom, a fantasy, a fiction.

For the money that is used in the world today, as we have seen, is not money at all. It does not exist. If it did exist, all those who have savings accounts at the bank and in insurance policies, etc., would be able to get their money. But it is an admitted fact that if all the people who have this money were at once to ask for it, not more than the first five or six out of a hundred could be served; 95 would go away empty-handed. *The money simply does not exist,* except in the imagination of the bankers and written down on some piece of paper.

We saw, in the state of Freedonia, that counterfeiters might steal from the state by adding to the money supply. The entire society would imagine that all this money existed. The same result could be reached if the politicians made it legal to create money. From the story of the Federal Reserve it is seen that the banks do exactly that. Money is lent to people on a "let's imagine" basis. This money was not owned by the bank in the first place, and it is not owned by the bank when it is paid off. What the bank does get is the interest. It creates an interest-bearing phantom. When the loan is paid off, that money goes out of existence again.

So it is clear that the owners of savings accounts do not own all that money; because it does not exist. The banks do not own it, because it does not exist. It is a pretense invented for the purpose of earning interest. And the Federal Reserve was given the right to "imagine" such money into existence and to reap interest.

So the lending itself is fictitious; and it is a pretense, for there is no such money. There was not before. And there will not be when it is paid back.

Now it becomes quite clear why the debt economy requires nonreduction of debt. For, you see, when people pay off their debts they are canceling out the money supply that was created when the loan was made to them. There is no greater horror for the modern government economists than the thought that people might wish, in volume, to pay off their debts—the money supply would disappear.

This must be abundantly clear to anyone watching television. Hardly an hour passes but some huckster bombards the audience with schemes to borrow money, and urges the borrower to spend now and pay later.

Continually increasing debt is a built-in mechanism of our credit-money system. Whenever the debt stops increasing, the system has to stop advancing. Already we have gone too far.

It is as though you were driving a car down a steep and icy mountain road. You are going 40 miles an hours, and you have a mile to go. If you put on the brakes you will go spinning over the cliff. If you don't put on the brakes you will be going so fast that you will end up a junk heap at the bottom of the road. Your mistake was that you got going at that speed on this road in the first place. It is too late now for you to rectify the situation. The further down the road you travel, the icier it gets and the steeper it gets—and already you dare not touch the brakes.

This is a true analogy to the credit-money system. I do not believe it can be successfully denied or refuted.

We are in this now and, for this reason, the only money that will count after we arrive at the climax will be the real money that is gold and silver; and, of course, all real things. But most real things are too bulky to hold and to store. Or they spoil with the weather. Or they shrink, or they decay. Or they are not quickly exchangeable. The only real money that is totally convenient, totally indestructible, and totally defensible, because it can be hidden and held, is gold and silver and the coins of each.

Cash should not be overlooked. It will be king if the money supply is sufficiently reduced by deflation and bankruptcy. This would make the surviving dollars worth *more* in terms of goods, but cash lodged in banks or bonds might end up on the casualty rather than survivor list.

25

SILVER

Any book on monetary affairs that did not include a section on silver would have to be called a cripple.

If you relate silver to gold, the first thing you note is the value ratio.

For thousands of years—from 450 B.C. until A.D. 1875—one ounce of gold was generally worth 15 to 16 ounces of silver. That was the low for silver, not the high. In the year A.D. 200 you could buy an ounce of gold with only ten ounces of silver, and in 3500 B.C., three ounces of silver were equal to one ounce of gold.

For 5,000 years, before silver had material and industrial uses, it held a consistently high value in relation to gold.

This relationship was upset by the development of the phenomenal Comstock Lode just before the turn of the century. Then silver dropped briefly during the Depression to where it took 70 ounces of silver to buy an ounce of gold.

But notice the quick rise of the silver curve to a ratio of 27:1 when the United States Treasury fixed silver at $1.30 an ounce while gold was fixed at $35 per ounce.

In 1967 the U.S. Treasury lost control of silver and the price rose to $2.50 per ounce, which placed silver once again near the historic ratio of 15:1.

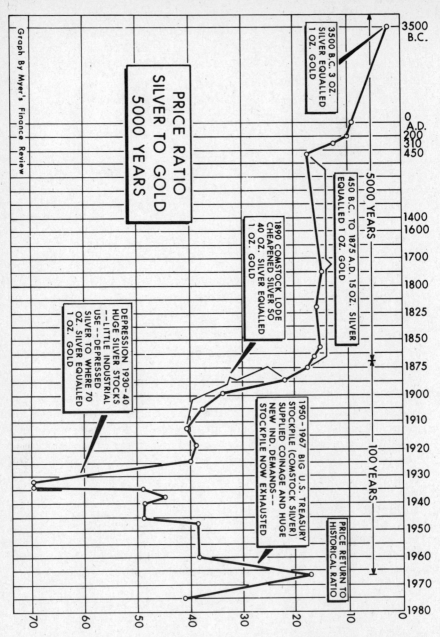

PRICE RATIO
SILVER TO GOLD
5000 YEARS

3500 B.C. 3 OZ. SILVER EQUALLED 1 OZ. GOLD

450 B.C. TO 1875 A.D. 15 OZ. SILVER EQUALLED 1 OZ. GOLD

1890 COMSTOCK LODE CHEAPENED SILVER SO 40 OZ. SILVER EQUALLED 1 OZ. GOLD

DEPRESSION 1930–40 HUGE SILVER STOCKS – LITTLE INDUSTRIAL USE – DEPRESSED SILVER TO WHERE 70 OZ. SILVER EQUALLED 1 OZ. GOLD

1950–1967 BIG U.S. TREASURY STOCKPILE (COMSTOCK SILVER) SUPPLIED COINAGE AND HUGE NEW IND. DEMANDS – STOCKPILE NOW EXHAUSTED

PRICE RETURN TO HISTORICAL RATIO

5000 YEARS

100 YEARS

3500 B.C.

0 A.D.
200
310
450

1400
1600
1700
1800
1825
1850
1875
1900
1910
1920
1930
1940
1950
1960
1970
1980

70 60 50 40 30 20 10 0

The above chart shows that the ratio of the price of silver to gold has now returned to the historic level that existed almost uninterruptedly from 450 B.C. to 1875 A.D. Development of the phenomenal Comstock Lode flooded the world market with silver so that by 1912 it had dropped to half its price in relation to gold. Since there was little industrial usage, silver was a drug on the market. The Great Depression of 1930–40 almost cut the silver price in half again. War usage of silver, plus the electronics revolution, consumed the silver at an alarming rate, exhausting the 2-billion-oz. stockpile between 1958 and 1967. While uses continue to multiply, production remains steady, resulting in an annual *demand deficit* of about 80% more than production.

During the turbulent times since 1967 both gold and silver have been moving violently. Silver, in 1975, was selling at a ratio of about 10:1 if related to the ridiculous price of gold as maintained by the U.S. Treasury. In actual fact, silver has been moving in the area of around 40:1, with gold at $176.00.

There are some very strong reasons why this ratio is seriously out of whack, and why it will be increasingly out of whack until the price rises. The facts weigh heavily in favor of a smaller ratio and thus a higher silver price. Here are some of the facts:

(1) When the U.S. Treasury sold half a billion ounces of silver at less than $2 an ounce—the price of gold was only $35 and the ratio was around *seventeen to one*.

(2) None of the world's treasuries now have any silver to dispose of. There is no *official stockpile* anywhere in the world.

(3) While gold rose from $35 to $175 an ounce—a 400 to 500 percent increase—silver rose from $1.30 per ounce to the present $4.20 per ounce—a little over a *threefold increase*. A fourfold increase would make silver $5.20 per ounce, and a fivefold increase would make silver $6.50 per ounce.

(4) The world's stocks and the rate of usage also seem to favor silver. There may be as much as 8 billion ounces of silver in the world—that's probably the maximum. There are 2 billion ounces of gold in the world —or a little more—and half of it is in the central banks. So there is only four times as much silver as there is gold. Additionally, the silver is being used—actually consumed—while gold, for the most part, mainly changes its form. For example, one-half to two-thirds of the industrially consumed gold has gone into jewelry, where it still exists as gold. The reason for that has been the fading confidence in the currencies. Once the currencies are stabilized, this industrial use of gold will drop off quickly; and the production of gold will be found to exceed greatly the industrial usage. And that is the difference. With gold it's *usage*. With silver it's mainly *consumption*.

In net result we face declining availability of silver, while in the long term we do not face declining availability of gold, at least to nearly the same extent. The exhaustion of the supplies of silver are foreseeable, whereas the exhaustion of the supplies of gold—apart from monetary usage—are not foreseeable.

(5) The world's shortfall of production of more than 100 million ounces a year since 1968 has been catching up. The shortfall has been minimized by (a) sales of speculators, (b) coinage melt and silver from India, (c) reclaimed silver, and (d) drawing on the stocks of silver.

Probably the predominant factor in the market on silver during the past two or three years has been speculator sales. The immense popularity of silver, when it first broke loose from Treasury control, resulted in massive speculator purchases. These were later liquidated as a result of the fall of the price from above $6 per ounce to below $4 per ounce. It may well be true that the speculative acquisition of gold during 1974 exceeded the net acquisition of speculative silver—proportionate to the price. In other words, gold has been enjoying a period of enormous popularity. Silver popularity has been moderate.

Those are the principal arguments favoring silver, and they have not fundamentally changed for a long time. In my book *Silver* (1969), I speculated that because of the strategic uses of silver, and because of its shortage, the price ratio would fall sometime to at least 10:1. On the 1975 market that would yield a silver price of $14 to $17 per ounce. At that time I did not expect a higher price than $100 per ounce for gold—and I speculated that silver would eventually reach $10 per ounce several years down the line. I thought that $6 per ounce was not at all unreasonable along with the price of gold. Silver did reach $6 per ounce—which at that time seemed fantastic—but of course it reached $6 later than I thought it would. However the long run picture has not changed as between silver and gold.

I think we are approaching the point where the pent-up discrepancies between these two metals will begin to exert themselves–and as usual will probably go too far in favor of silver. I don't know how far this is, but it's a long way up from here.

From a technical standpoint, we must observe that silver has been above $6 and, if it is in an uptrend, will again go beyond $6. Psychologically, from having observed the market for a long time, I have noticed that there are certain strong areas of price resistance. One dollar, on any quotation, is a mark of strong resistance. Each hundred dollars up to $500 is a mark of strong resistance, and $500 is particularly strong.

Whether it be $5 or $500 matters not. If silver breaks through $5 and sells well there and holds above there, the next strong resistance point is $7.50. I have never seen $6 to be a strong resistance point, or $6.50. But $7.50 is not nearly as strong a resistance point as $5.

I believe that the next time silver goes on a bender it will pass $7.50. Silver has shown itself to be a fast performer. Everytime in the past when it has gone up, it has gone up very fast. It is just as fast a performer on the downside. I don't think it would be unreasonable to expect silver to pass $7 in 1976. But, two influences could work against that:

(1) If the price of gold were to drop materially, one would expect to see a weakness in silver.

(2) A severe world depression would cut down on the usage. *However remember*—when that happens there will be a big decline in the mining of copper, zinc, and all silver-related materials, so that the production

of silver would fall accordingly. The shortfall of usage against production would still be very large.

And remember this: *The stocks of silver are not inexhaustible.* We tend to forget that. We tend to forget how near the point we may be to when we arrive at that crunch. A bit of a silver corner developed in the spring of 1974. That was not the real silver corner because it was largely man-made. The big silver corner will come when the supplies, regardless of anyone, just are not meeting the demand. When that times arrives $10 will be a low price for silver. Another element that well may enter the scene in 1976 is the fact that gold is so high priced that ordinary people can only buy tiny quantities of it. There may be a growing tendency for people to save silver as a hedge of last resort on the level of the common man, whereas the sheikhs save gold.

At any rate—the *potential* of silver now would appear to be considerably greater than the potential of gold. Since it has been riding in a fairly stable area between $4 and $5 (that's psychologically like gold between $40 and $50—and you know how long it stayed there) and that certainly is not a large percentage fluctuation—*overall* it would appear to me that this area, particularly around $4.50, is highly favorable for the purchase of silver. And what applies to silver must apply to the best silver stocks.

It can be taken for granted that metals are safer than other commodities, but are not necessarily a good investment at any given time. They are safer than other commodities for the simple reason that they won't spoil. Sugar can get damp and cake; grain can mold; eggs and tomatoes will get rotten; but metals can be safely held for almost any length of time. Other than that, metals must be measured, just like anything else, by the growing or lagging desirability of the metal as prescribed by economic factors.

Only gold and silver stand apart from the other metals, and have so stood for thousands of years. That's not likely to change. The other precious metals will be priced according to the conditions. For example, platinum will remain rare, but if its usage fails to meet expectations, the price will decline. The fact that the world is going into a depression, and the price of platinum has been based on forecasts of a huge new industry of pollution control, may very well erode the price of platinum. Diamonds, which may be in much less demand due to strained economies, may fall in price, and probably will. All of the other metals fall into the same category. Of course if war or other unforeseen restrictions prevent the import of a scarce metal—that metal will go up, just as oil went up under those conditions.

Gold and silver, however, are the metal stand-bys for those who would preserve their wealth.

Working strongly in favor of silver is a relative decline in silver

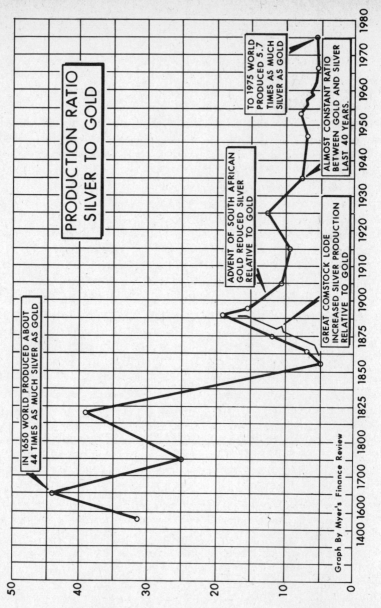

PRODUCTION RATIO
SILVER TO GOLD

IN 1650 WORLD PRODUCED ABOUT 44 TIMES AS MUCH SILVER AS GOLD

ADVENT OF SOUTH AFRICAN GOLD REDUCED SILVER RELATIVE TO GOLD

GREAT COMSTOCK LODE INCREASED SILVER PRODUCTION RELATIVE TO GOLD

TO 1975 WORLD PRODUCED 5.7 TIMES AS MUCH SILVER AS GOLD

ALMOST CONSTANT RATIO BETWEEN GOLD AND SILVER LAST 40 YEARS.

Graph By Myer's Finance Review

1400 1600 1700 1800 1825 1850 1875 1900 1910 1920 1930 1940 1950 1960 1970 1980

50 40 30 20 10 0

production compared with gold production. It has declined drastically in the last 200 years.

In 1650 the world was producing 44 times as much silver as gold. But now it only produces about five times as much silver as gold.

Yet all this time the consumption of silver far outstripped the consumption of gold. So that, while the supply of gold—once the monetary

166

situation is stabilized—can remain adequate for at least a generation, this is not true of silver. The shortfall of production over consumption continues, even under recession conditions.

It is very important to remember that, in a depression, production from copper and zinc mines will be seriously curtailed. That means an automatic curtailment of 80 percent of the source material of silver production—because nearly 80 percent of silver is mined in conjunction with copper and zinc and other metals. To increase silver production substantially, production of those other metals would have to be increased. While a depression would cut down on the consumption of silver, and the shortfall would remain intact.

So every month, month after month, year after year, we are eating away at the remaining store of silver.

The outlook is that the demand will grow much greater. The world must move away from pollution. Silver holds out one of the great promises not only in the control of pollution but in the huge upcoming area of batteries. As technology advances, the consumption picture for silver advances. Today photography consumes most of the silver, but tomorrow electronics and other new technologies may rival photography in their demand.

At the same time, silver is still money—regardless of what the Central Banks say. We know this because we know there are several hundred million dollars in silver holdings that plainly state on the face of them that they are money—and which are accepted without question as money—and, what is more, a money that constantly appreciates in value. It is easily proven—a silver quarter of 1967 is worth nearly a dollar today, and during the spring of 1974 was worth quite a bit more than a dollar. Who would have believed it?

I think silver still has a monetary role to play—and in this manner. How many average people can go in and buy a 20-ounce bar of gold— a 10-ounce bar—and how many can buy a one-ounce bar at one hundred and forty dollars plus the premium? Nor are the scores of millions of working class people likely to be satisfied to hold this little one-ounce bar. They would find it hard to negotiate for their needs. The sum is too large in one chunk. Gold is the monetary Gibraltar for the larger sums of money, and for the very rich. I believe that silver still has a role to play as the monetary Gibraltar of the millions who cannot spend very much on total security—but still can spend something to know that they will have money that will always work.

And so I repeat—it is not unreasonable to think that in the not-too-distant future silver, instead of selling at a ratio of 16 to one for gold, may well sell more like ten to one for gold—as the uses of silver continue to increase, and the shortfall is accentuated.

I believe that when the right day comes the correction in the silver price will be even more dramatic than it was in gold. I believe the rising curve of silver will be breathtaking. I believe the big move has been seen in gold, but the big move remains to be seen in silver.

Whether this will happen in 1976, I do not know. But I do not believe that it will be later than 1978. The stocks of silver are growing low—and it is beginning to show.

Here was the situation in silver in the spring of 1975:

The world produced 240 million ounces and consumed 448 million ounces. The United States alone consumed 190 million ounces, down about only 4 million ounces from 1973.

Two large copper mines, Newmont Magna and Inspiration Copper, cut their production, materially reducing the outlook for silver production in 1975. If the recession deepened, there would be more cuts in production.

The supply of silver above ground is not large. The U.S. Bureau of the Mint lists it as 30 million ounces as of December 31, 1974. Not all that 30 million ounces is available. Over 7 million ounces are in the channels of being processed by the silver refiners.

So with 23 million ounces to draw on, and the United States alone using more than 15 million ounces a month, the immediate visible supply is for only about two months.

Of course there are the warehouse stocks. This amounts to about 90 million ounces.

However, this stock cannot be considered to be available at the snap of a finger. This stock is all owned by someone. Some of it is owned, or can be called upon, by the silver refiners. Much of it is owned by speculators, sometimes more respectably called investors. The price at which it will be sold is a big question mark. If silver should get really scarce, it could be that the strong speculators holding silver would not sell at all—particularly under the threat of war or worsening world monetary conditions. Or it could be that they would sell only at a very high price.

It could also be that they would let loose at a lower price. But I do not see many reasons for this.

About 200 million ounces will be produced in the Western Hemisphere in 1975, and that is enough to look after the needs of the United States. But no more than 240 million ounces will be produced worldwide, and other countries in the world use cameras too; and are engaged in electronics and pollution control.

The supply situation is not completely critical, but it is moving in that direction.

Over and above the visible supplies of silver mentioned above we have a certain amount of storage by bullion dealers in England and

Switzerland. No one knows how much that is, but it is considered to be rather smaller than the American speculative supplies. The acquisition of silver has not been popular in the last few years, and much of the silver held in London and Zurich is in long-term hands.

Beyond that we have some hundreds of millions of ounces in United States coinage. Coins nearly always carry a premium over metal. A certain amount of coinage is melted down, but smelters are not getting very large supplies from coinage; and if silver is increasingly looked upon as a "store of value," they will get less and less of the coinage for the melting pots. Or if they do get it, they will have to pay a higher and higher price.

Probably the largest supply of silver is in India, but there it is held in tiny amounts in the form of jewelry by scores of millions of peasants holding it for a last-ditch emergency.

All in all, the future for silver is subject to more influences than probably any other commodity, and certainly to more factors than gold. But whatever happens over the short term, one must not lose sight of the three major factors as far as silver is concerned.

(1) The shortfall is about a hundred million ounces a year.

(2) Silver is being consumed—not stored like gold.

(3) Sooner or later the well is going to run dry, and we are not too far away from that day. When that day comes there could be a panic to buy silver, and a ratio of ten to one is a fairly reasonable expectation.

WHAT THIS MEANS TO YOU

This means that you take absolutely no risk in holding silver coinage. It is a protection against any kind of monetary or economic adversity. It will always have buying power. Whatever happens to paper money, silver will be a solid reserve.

That means that no one should be without a supply of silver coinage that would serve him in time of need, whether it arise from a ruined currency or riots in the streets. Everyone should have silver for use in emergencies—silver to buy groceries—silver to buy lodgings, clothing, an airplane ticket. Rich and poor alike should have some reserve of silver coinage.

The rich may buy in bags at $3500 each. The poor may buy it for their piggy banks. But everyone should have it.

26

THE STOCK MARKET—
INVESTMENT MANIA

A large part of the evil of inflation arises from the need to keep pace with it. Those who do not put their money on a vehicle that runs as fast as the inflation find the value of their money depreciating. It's no wonder, therefore, that an inflationary era of 30-years duration produced the phenomena of the greatest bull market and the longest bull market in history.

Past periods of inflation had been relatively short-lived. That was because it was impossible to sustain them against a background of real money. The invention of the gold-exchange standard, and the circulation of debt certificates in place of money, provided the authorities with facilities to keep the inflationary machine running.

Previously, injections of *real* money would have been necessary to keep the inflationary machine alive. Since such money did not exist, the overheated economy had to come to its senses. This always had a sobering effect on the stock market and, usually, a severe although not disastrous correction.

Under the debt economy—under circumstances where debt served as money—injections of new money became relatively easy. All you had to do was to increase the debt. Presto! There was the new money.

From the end of World War II until 1966 the stock market enjoyed its greatest and longest boom. Except for corrections here and there, the curve of the Dow Jones was steadily and inexorably up. And as it rose its speed of acceleration increased.

By the early 1960s inflation was beginning to be recognized by all. Brokers were quick to point out to their clients that if they left their money in cash its quality would be gradually eroded. However, they said, if clients invested their money in stocks, the stocks would rise along with the inflation, and, in the case of very good stocks, would outpace the inflation.

This popular type of buying during the sixties was fundamentally different from the investments made in our colony of Freedonia. As we understood it then, when we had real money we might invest our savings in, say, a shoe factory if we foresaw a rising market for shoes, and if the factory was run by a good manager and staff, with excellent cobblers. Our idea was that the true wealth of this business would increase, and that we would share in it.

The investment by the public in the 1960s was made for quite a different reason. Most of the buying was based not so much on visions of increased wealth of the business as on the judgment that other people would pay more for the stock later, regardless of what it was worth. Growth became a magic word. A reasonable expectation on earnings from share investments had been 10 percent. Now people bought stocks not at a cost of ten times earnings, but often 40 times earnings, 80 times earnings, 100 times earnings; on the theory that other people would get so excited about the prospects of these stocks that they would pay 120 times earnings and would take these stocks off the hands of the present buyer at a profit to him. The investment idea, as it had been traditionally known, became increasingly distorted. Investment gave way to speculation. Speculation gave way to outright gambling.

This kind of a market emanated from two fundamentals of human nature. One was fear; the other greed. People bought for fear that the value of their savings would disappear as a result of inflation, unless they changed cash into stocks. They bought from greed once they saw what other people were making at this marvellous new game.

Essentially, though, the massive buying by the American public rose out of fear, which itself arose from inflation. Really, without being aware of it, people were running from money.

The first factor that every investor in the stock market should take account of, before he buys, is the overhanging weight of potential selling. This is true whether you are dealing in a small mining stock, a massive stock like General Motors, or the spectrum of stocks across the total economy, which is assumed to be measured by an index known as the "Dow Jones Average." Any smart stock market operator knows that the time to buy the shares of a company is before it has become highly popular. The reason for this is that once it has become very popular, large numbers of former stockholders are potential sellers when it makes a healthy rise. This overhang of potential sellers is "bearish."

The point is that the more people who are involved for the simple reason of making a profit, the nearer we are to the top. In order for the stock to hold even, there will have to be an army of new buyers coming along just as optimistic about the future as the previous army of buyers. In order for the stock to go up, this new army will have to be bigger than the army of potential sellers. Obviously, somewhere along the line, the newest army of buyers will be smaller than the preceding army, which has by now become the "selling" army. Then we will have more sellers than buyers, and the stock will go down. This is true also for the entire mass of the stock market.

The alternating size of these two armies determines whether the stock market will go up or down. It is strictly a question of psychology. One might stretch that to say it is strictly a question of fashionable thinking. It is true that the fashionable thinking rests largely on the net overall judgment of business activity. But there is another factor that has nothing to do with the truth. The fashionable psychology can be the result of propaganda. Since the investment public tends to move on the herd instinct, even a sustained move in the Dow Jones can be entirely misconceived.

Charts try to measure what people are doing. That is, what people have been thinking, what they are continuing to think, and, therefore, what they will likely continue to do. Charts are very valuable in this respect.

But charts cannot shed the faintest ray of light on whether or not what people are doing is solidly or falsely based. If the move is falsely based, of course, that will be found out sooner or later. Then the market will go into the reverse direction.

In other words, the market is blind. It makes me think of a blind monster trying to get out of a maze. He rumbles along in one direction and, as long as he runs into no great obstacles, continues until he smashes his head against a wall. Then he turns and rumbles in the other direction until he hits another wall.

How else can you interpret the movement of the Dow Jones from 1965 right through 1975? Look at the graph in this chapter. You must conclude that most of the moves of the Dow Jones were purposeless— except for one thing. The blind monster never, throughout all this time, took inflation into account.

The inflation meant that the Dow Jones was not doing at all what it seemed to be doing. While it was going up it was all the time really going down, so that when it hit the thousand mark in mid-1968, and again in mid-1972, it was nowhere near the mark of a thousand that it had reached in 1965. When it reached the peak of a thousand in 1972, inflation had destroyed more than one-third of it. It was really around 650.

The blind monster and the blind followers of the monster on Wall Street never tumbled to the fact that the whole thing amounted to the most massive bear market in the history of the world. Either they wouldn't see, or they didn't want to see that the great recovery of 1972 meant that all the massive billions invested had depreciated by at least one-third. To be even, the market would have had to rise to 1350.

Throughout all the ten-year period, the fluctuations of the Dow Jones were really a measure of changing psychology—first optimistic, then pessimistic. It was a measure of the size of the two armies, the pessimists and the optimists. There was a seesaw battle between the size of these armies. And it must be said that neither of these armies displayed any intelligent insight as to the direction in which the world was marching.

When it became fashionable to accept the cliche "We have to live with inflation, and the way to do it is to buy stocks"— when that became almost a public fetish, the army of people holding stocks assumed massive proportions. By 1966 the army of people owning stocks far outnumbered the army of people still wanting stocks.

I don't pretend here to go into all the causes of the crash of 1966, but this was certainly a major one.

The Dow Jones averages dropped from a January reading of 1001 to a May reading of 735. It was by no means a measure of the percentage losses to the general public. The damage to the Dow Jones industrials—considered to be the big blue chips—was small compared to the depreciation in many of the speculative stocks, the growth stocks, the glamour stocks, the cat-and-dog stocks. The public took a severe beating. The big public never really returned to the market in force. It had lost confidence in its ability to invest in the right stock.

The market was turned around by injections of new money, but the self-confidence of the army of individual investors had been damaged. The climate was ready for the stellar performance of the mutual funds. Their salesmen penetrated every nook and cranny of the land.

The pitch was this: "You've been hurt in the market, sure. But why have you been hurt? You have been hurt because you have gone into a game that you do not have the background to understand. In our office we have analysts who spend their entire days examining investments. We have the finest brains out of Harvard and Yale, and our firm can draw on the expert eyes of experienced operators with proven judgment. On top of this we can apply the magic art of the computer. How could you expect to make money as an amateur against these experts? Now we offer you these services. You will pay a larger commission to buy the stocks if you do so through us. But it will give you a service that would be cheap at twice the price."

The public went for that.

The need to keep up with inflation was greater than ever. The experts would be their employees. These experts with their noses to the grindstone, pouring over sets of tables from morning to night, would come up with the right answers, and we the investors would reap the profit.

And that worked pretty well for a while.

The investing public poured its money into the mutual funds and other institutional forms, which bought up large volumes of stocks and put new life in the market, with the result that the Dow Jones launched a rather dramatic recovery.

But now we had a new situation. The market had traded the sensitivity of feeling of the many (the public) for the feelings of the few (the experts). The feelings of the many are grass roots. The feelings—the optimism or the pessimism—of the few are academic.

By 1970 mutual funds and institutions had replaced the volume of injection of money that previously had come from millions of individuals. And whereas at one time the public accounted for 80 percent of the trading, now 80 percent was being done by institution managers.

President Nixon had decided that he would fight inflation. Apparently he did not understand that the new debt economy was like a bicycle that had to be kept in motion. If you ever stopped going forward in the process of increasing debt, your bicycle lost its momentum and, losing that momentum, would fall down. Within five months, from January 1970 to May, the Dow Jones thermometer plummeted from 995 to a new low of 631. It was a near disaster.

In the midst of the panic, two of the largest firms in the United States stood helpless before the yawning jaws of bankruptcy. In the case of Lockheed, the Bank of America was in so deep that the bankruptcy of Lockheed would almost certainly spell bankruptcy for the Bank of America. The bankruptcy of that bank, and its consequently necessary calling of loans, would set off a chain reaction that might easily result in a total collapse of liquidity.

As if that weren't enough, Penn Central Railway, one of the world's industrial giants, informed Congress that if it didn't get help immediately it would also have to declare receivership.

After emergency meetings, it was announced that the government would probably stand behind both Lockheed and Penn Central. They called out the Chairman of the Federal Reserve System, Arthur Burns; and he told the country there would be no shortage of liquidity. What Arthur Burns really said was this: "However much money may be needed, count on us to make it available." That turned the tide of the market again. In six months it sprinted from its May low of 635 to launch an assault on its old 1966 high of 1000. It got as far as 951.

By 1975, we had a different story. Mr. Burns was trying to expand the money supply and couldn't make it work. In February he testified before a congressional committee that in spite of efforts to increase the money supply by 6 percent or more it had actually fallen. We shall speak about this later, but it is injected at this point to show that, when inflation is nearing its end, increasing the money supply by the debt mechanism is not as simple as it sounds. While inflation is going, every offering of money by the Fed is eagerly pulled away. When inflation is about to fail, the Fed finds itself pushing a string. Eager borrowers are in financial trouble and are not wanted. Worthy borrowers, fearing to expand, don't want the money.

But back in 1970 all offerings of money were quickly snapped up, and the market reacted like an injected filly.

As late as 1973, counting a population of something more than 200 million, and assuming that half are under- or over-age, practically one out of every three employed persons was still an investor directly in the market, with an additional unknown quantity involved in one way or another through the institutions.

Probably half or more of the public of the United States was in the stock market. Was it possible to expect that the other half were going to be buyers after witnessing the unhappy experience of their friends over a period since 1966?

The age of inflation had coaxed the maximum public into the stock market. There were not enough people left on the outside of the fence to rescue those already inside. We were witnessing the transformation of the psychology of public investment. But it was generally not perceived by the investment wizards on Wall Street until too late.

The next time the sellers got scared, the Dow went to 627 in 1970. Again, in 1973, those who were "bullish on America" jumped in. The herd instinct took over, and in early 1973 the market roared up past a thousand. From then on, with some wild fluctuations, it was a downhill road to the low point of 576 in late 1974.

Once again the dumb blind giant turned around, and we had the explosive rally of early 1975.

No one stopped to think that even if this rally should reach as high as a thousand it would still only be 600 compared with the Dow Jones standing of 1965—because of depreciation by inflation.

The bull market actually had lasted from the early 1950s through 1965. *The factor of inflation meant that the market would have to go past 1600 in 1975 before it could be said to have recovered lost ground.*

Throughout these recoveries a very important element was being overlooked. Each recovery showed the volume to be more the work of institutions and less the volume of John Q. Public. Each of the recoveries showed more block trading than the previous ones. And most of the stock market, indeed, was being handled by the big fund managers.

If public investment was going out of fashion, so was the stock market.

Another pillar in our era—the era of credit—was beginning to crack. The warning was being flashed by growing bankruptcies.

Bankruptcies always lag behind the reality of the bankruptcy. Bankruptcy is the final *admission*. In 1974 we had the bankruptcies that were building up in 1973. The most notable was the Franklin National Bank —the eighth largest in the United States.

The dethroned millionaire was asked: "How did you go bankrupt?" He replied: "Gradually for quite a while—then all at once!"

The bankruptcies being registered in 1975 were about five times as many as those in 1974.

Few of the American brokerage houses connected the sickness of the New York Stock Exchange with the international monetary situation. Nevertheless, that was where the immediate cause lay. The lack of confidence in the dollar had swelled the reserves of foreign countries. That capital had fled to foreign treasuries because it feared a devaluation of the dollar. If it resided in a strong currency that loss would be avoided. The capital flow proved to be correct. President Nixon devalued the dollar 10 percent, the second devaluation in 14 months.

Perhaps the surest sign of trouble, even in 1973, was a psychological phenomenon that a sharp farmer with a grade-five education might view with suspicion. It was the overdone brokerage proclamation: "We're bullish on America!"

This slogan had found wide usage about the time of the crash of 1929. When the stock market is sound and healthy, supporting slogans are superfluous. During the great bull market of 1946 to 1966 no one heard these pseudopatriotic announcements. But in the spring of 1973 the large brokerage institutions were running advertisements almost daily emphasizing their "Bullishness on America."

Even the New York Stock Exchange was running ads urging the public to get in and take advantage of the anticipated growth in the business of America.

And in January of 1975, General Motors ran large ads proclaiming that it was patriotic to "buy a car"—implying that it was unpatriotic not

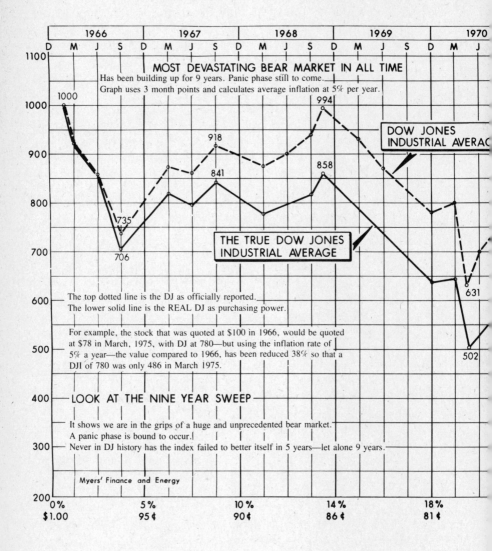

MOST DEVASTATING BEAR MARKET IN ALL TIME

Has been building up for 9 years. Panic phase still to come.
Graph uses 3 month points and calculates average inflation at 5% per year.

DOW JONES
INDUSTRIAL AVERAG

THE TRUE DOW JONES
INDUSTRIAL AVERAGE

The top dotted line is the DJ as officially reported.
The lower solid line is the REAL DJ as purchasing power.

For example, the stock that was quoted at $100 in 1966, would be quoted
at $78 in March, 1975, with DJ at 780—but using the inflation rate of
5% a year—the value compared to 1966, has been reduced 38% so that a
DJI of 780 was only 486 in March 1975.

LOOK AT THE NINE YEAR SWEEP

It shows we are in the grips of a huge and unprecedented bear market.
A panic phase is bound to occur.
Never in DJ history has the index failed to better itself in 5 years—let alone 9 years.

Myers' Finance and Energy

| 0% | 5% | 10% | 14% | 18% |
| $1.00 | 95¢ | 90¢ | 86¢ | 81¢ |

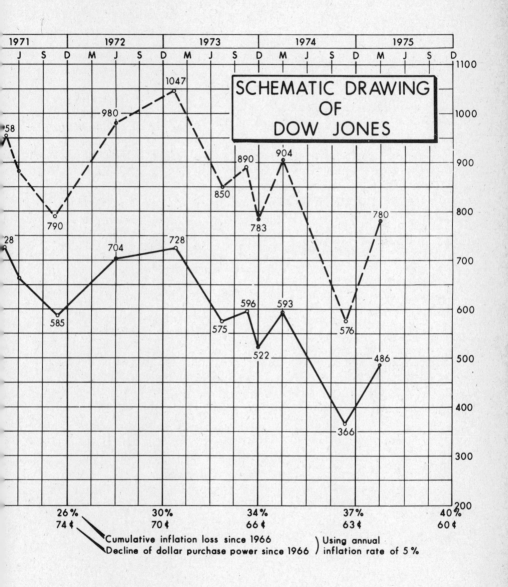

SCHEMATIC DRAWING
OF
DOW JONES

179

to buy a car. All red-blooded Americans who could afford it ought to pitch in and buy cars. It was like the wartime slogan, "Buy a bond today."

When, in April 1973 (with the Dow around 900), I predicted that the stock market would be lucky if it could bottom out in the 500 to 600 range in 1974, I was regarded not only as a nut, but the worst kind of a nut—a false prophet of gloom and doom. *Barron's* magazine headlined me as the "BEAR FROM THE NORTH."

But I noticed—didn't you?—that before the end of 1974 the Dow Jones actually did hit 576.

I made this assessment not on the basis of charts or great technical knowledge, but rather on the basis of psychological considerations. The most important of these was the price/earnings ratio.

If a stock earns $10 a year and is selling on the market at $100, it is said to have a price/earnings ratio of ten. The price/earnings ratio is therefore a measurement of the buoyancy factor in the investment community. When the future looks good, people are willing to credit the stocks with a larger factor of growth. When the future looks bleak they are apt to move to the extreme in the other direction. We have had price/earnings ratios of up to 20 for the Dow Jones averages as a whole. We have had them down as low as six. In the spring of 1973 they had fallen from their high of 19 seven years before to 13. It showed that investors were becoming increasingly uncertain about growth. If they should become downright pessimistic, the figure could drop to ten or eight or even six. There is no rule as to what a price/earnings ratio should be. Although the brokers seem to assume that the market is required to be reasonable, there is no requirement on the stock market.

But a reduction in the effective price/earnings ratio is quite a lot more serious than a change that might develop from reduced earnings.

If, for example, General Motors earns $6 a year, and if it is selling at $78 a share, it is being given a price/earnings ratio of 13.

A poor year might bring General Motors down to $5 in earnings. If the price/earnings ratio persisted it would drop only to $65 per share. *But if, at the same time, a generally depressive psychology resulted in a bleaker outlook for the future, and if the price/earnings ratio were to drop to ten, the price of General Motors would recede to $50 per share.* If the earnings dropped to four—which they could in time of serious recession—the tendency would be for the price/earnings ratio to drop as well. If the price/earnings ratio dropped to eight—the price of General Motors would be $32 per share.

Well, when I made that assessment in *Myers' Finance & Energy*, General Motors was in the $60 area, and it looked simply absurd. But I noticed—didn't you?—that General Motors actually hit 29 in the low of 1974.

Every bear market has its early period of erosion and its dramatic period of drop; then followed by another period of erosion. To me it appeared that the unusually long bull market from 1946 to 1966 had become a bear market with an unusually long first-stage erosional period (1966-1975) that was on the verge of being transformed into the second-stage dramatic slide.

But always to be added to this massive fall is the deduction for the comparative inflation.

When the distortions become serious, international traders find themselves increasingly restricted. A large oil tanker may take three years to build. How can a contract be drawn on the delivery price when the currencies are moving around like jumping beans? This puts another brake on the Dow Jones, regardless of its violent short-term convulsions.

The multiplication of the distortions themselves project the end of the age of inflation from the mere fact that the vision of economic communicators becomes blurred to the point where they can no longer perform. That leads to a collapse of international business, which leads to a collapse of business at home—which, in the circumstances of mountains of credit, can only lead to economic collapse and the total collapse of the market.

The collapse of the currency (deflation) under the circumstances now threatening us can only signal the end of a way of life—a social era where debt is preferable to credit, where thrift is silly, where savers become suckers, where spenders make off with the loot, where debtors end up with the property of their creditors, and where the basic values by which the economies of the world have advanced are turned upside down.

That truly comprises an era. The stock market action was a part and a manifestation of that era of expecting something for nothing and of a worldwide attempt to create something from nothing (inflation).

27

PUTTING IT ALL TOGETHER— BRINGING IT INTO FOCUS

We have covered a lot of ground and some apparently disassociated subjects. However, every subject covered is intimately related with every other subject, and properly put together they produce a single clear picture.

You should now be in a position to see this picture in distinct focus. The elements we have to consider are as follows:

(1) The monetary crisis.

(2) The currency crisis.

(3) The energy crisis.

(4) The investment crisis (stock market and bonds).

(5) The labor crisis.

(6) The food crisis (this has not been dealt with previously because it is not complicated, but it is becoming an increasingly vital part of the whole world picture).

THE MONETARY CRISIS

This crisis has been building up since 1968, when the world gold pool went broke. Although the dollar was theoretically convertible into gold by any country, the United States strongarmed all the nations of the Western world not to exchange the dollars they had earned for gold. The reason was that the U.S. gold pile had come down to a level of about $10 billion, which was apparently considered as the danger level by military and top political authorities.

As a consequence the world moved forward wearing illusionary glasses. It was loudly proclaimed that the dollar was as good as gold—in fact, it was better than gold—in fact, the only reason gold was worth anything at all was that the U.S. Treasury stood ready to redeem all dollars in gold. It put up a sign at the window, "Redeem your dollars for gold!"

But when you went to the window with some dollars and tentatively offered them in your hand, they slammed the window on your fingers. To each of the line-up of customers behind you they showed the sign, "Exchange your dollars for gold." After about three came out with smashed fingers—the rest stopped coming. No country was strong enough to challenge the United States; and so the pretense went on— "The dollar is as good as gold."

Relieved of the necessity of putting out gold for the dollars it spent abroad, the United States continued to manufacture huge amounts of money. It spent this money on the Vietnam war, and this money infiltrated itself into various countries. It spent it on troops in Germany. It spent it on massive imports of oil and other raw materials. And it spent it on manufactured products from other countries. But the dollars continued to pile up in the scores of billions in foreign treasuries. No one could get anything back for these dollars. Of course they could buy, if they wished: American Buicks and American television sets. But they did not want to buy these things. They wanted to make them in their own countries and sell them abroad. It amounted to dollar imperialism.

By 1971 the pressure had become so great that there was a threat of a massive exchange of dollars for gold. At that time President Nixon closed the gold window and ended the pretense that the dollar could be exchanged for gold.

Soon thereafter the world went on floating exchange rates. That is to say, no longer was one currency guaranteed by the central bank of a country to be worth an equivalent value of another currency, which was, in turn, worth a specified number of dollars. Currencies fluctuated like stocks on the stock market, according to the demand. Central banks tried to buy dollars when the dollar went too low in relation to their own currencies, because, if their currencies were too high, it made their exports to the United States too high and they couldn't sell anything. But still, for every dollar they bought, they had to issue more of their own currencies—thereby leaving themselves at the mercy of the inflation of the United States.

The United States was still spending much more than it was producing, and by 1975 it had piled up more than a hundred billion unredeemable dollars.

As these huge amounts of unusable dollars accumulated, the dollar continued to sink in relation to foreign currencies. The Arabs had found that their political move of embargoing oil during the Israeli war had worked. They had, collectively, an enormous power. Immediately they found this out, they challenged the U.S. dollar by raising the price of their oil 400 percent.

The effect was to create an even worse monetary crisis. The Arabs were now taking in billions of dollars. The U.S. deficit was growing. Arabs had no place to spend this money, because they only had small populations, and so these billions continued to accumulate in the treasuries of the oil-producing countries. This was like the comedy where you see the large doughnut machine running wildly all night in a small room, because someone has forgotten to turn it off—threatening to burst the walls of the room with doughnuts.

The debt of the United States was piling up to a mind-boggling figure: to such an extent, in fact, that no one, by early 1975, had any idea of how the monetary crisis was to be solved.

In my "Report from Switzerland," March 1975, I wrote the following:

MONETARY CONFUSION DEEPENS

On previous visits over the last several years one could always find suggested remedies. Desperate perhaps—far out perhaps—some of them doubtful, and verging on the implausible perhaps—but some kind of suggestion for a remedy to the world monetary situation.

On this visit I don't even hear suggestions.

In short, the situation has worsened so much and become so inextricably complicated and entangled that the best thinkers seem to me to have given up.

Two years ago, one would hear such specific pronouncements as: "The United States debt must be funded. Otherwise we are drifting hopelessly into chaos. We must fund the debt." Or you might hear, "The Common Market countries may form a currency of their own." Or you might even hear, "We shall have to return to gold at a much higher price—perhaps $100 or more." Or you might hear, "The SDR's will have to be activated—we shall have to get rid of gold."

On this visit I hear none of these. I hear no suggestions at all.

It is as though everyone has thrown up his hands.

"I asked the Chairman of the Board of one of the very largest banks in Switzerland or the world, "Will we go back to gold?" He said, "No, we will not go back to the gold standard."

I asked the chief economist of an equally large bank, "Will we go back to the gold standard?" He replied, "We will have to eventually go to gold. There is no other way."

I asked another banker, "How is the Arab oil money to be handled?" He said, "They will have to invest on the longer term. What else will they do with it?"

"But how?" I asked. "They're only investing on the short term."

"True," he said, "ninety days or six months. They are afraid of the currencies."

I asked, "Then what are they going to do with it?" He had no answer. It has to be done—but he had no answer.

I have no answer to the monetary crisis, and I don't know anyone who has. The whole world now is running on a bubble of credit and debt, and I can foresee nothing but the total collapse of money and an indescribable confusion and chaos.

I wouldn't be so pessimistic if during the past six years I had even seen an intelligent solution suggested—much less pursued. I have attended the conferences of the International Monetary Fund periodically since 1967—and I can say, in absolute truth, there has not been one bit of progress. We have suffered one retreat after another. Nothing has become any better. The situation has continued to worsen. This in spite of all the meetings, conferences, and proclamations of the finance ministers and the central bankers of the world.

My common sense makes me question—if they haven't been able to do anything to improve matters during all this time, what can they do now?

Of course there is one thing they could do, and that has been plain from the beginning. They could stabilize the money of the world. If they could stabilize money, the monetary crisis would go away at once.

But you see, the only way to stabilize money is to stop the excess issuing of money, and this excess issuing is largely in the hands of the United States. The United States will not cut down on its consumption of foreign imported oil, or other raw materials, and even refuses to draw in its horns in its vast enterprises around the world. At the same time, the politicians refuse to allow any reduction in the living standard because they know they would be thrown out in the next election.

If they went on the gold standard—reality would arrive tomorrow morning. This reality would be too horrible to contemplate.

Additionally, the return to the gold standard is now extremely difficult. Some countries, such as the European countries Germany, France, Switzerland, Italy, Holland, and Belgiuim, have not completely trusted the U.S. dollar and have retained their hoards of gold. They have more than $20 billion, even with gold valued at the old price of $35 an ounce.

But countries like Britain and Japan, and the developing countries, have completely trusted the American dollar, and all of their reserves are in American dollars that are continually depreciating.

If the world went on a gold standard, what happens to Japan and Britain—and if their Central Banks go completely bankrupt, what are the repercussions on the banks of the West to whom these banks also owe billions of dollars?

The problem is too complicated for me, and, as far as I can see, it is too complicated for any of the authorities or all of them combined. They simply don't know what to do.

In the end, of course, there will be a result and a resolution of these forces—just as there always is in nature. What we are facing very soon is another vast surge of inflation that will destroy all of the currencies. Or we are facing a massive deflation—that is to say, a wave of bankruptcies across the world that will wipe out dollars by the billions upon billions and scores of billions.

In other words, sooner or later the massive world debt will be liquidated. It will be liquidated either by default (bankruptcy and deflation), or it will be liquidated by devising a new currency in which you give one new dollar for five, ten, or 20—or whatever—of the old.

In the next chapter we shall briefly examine the likelihood of one or the other of these solutions.

So much for the monetary crisis.

THE CURRENCY CRISIS

Of course, the currency crisis rises immediately and quite simply from the monetary crisis. The currency crisis is mainly connected with the efforts of other countries to stop the inflow of dollars that forces them to inflate their own currencies whether they like it or not.

But it has been found practically impossible to bar the influx of dollars.

As explained earlier, the efforts of Switzerland have been the most extreme of all countries. They levied a 40-percent penalty on deposits of dollars if one changed them into Swiss francs and left them on deposit in a Swiss bank. In other words, if you put in a hundred dollars, you would end up with sixty at the end of the year (not actually on a small-deposit basis—but for any large sums).

One would think this was enough to stop you short.

The hundreds of Americans and other people in the world holding dollars wanted to change them into Swiss francs because the Swiss franc has more gold backing than any other currency in the world.

But Switzerland is only a small country. How could it possibly issue enough Swiss francs to accommodate the influx of billions upon billions of dollars. Already the inflation in Switzerland is shocking.

Where I paid $8 to get from the airport to the hotel in 1973, on my 1975 trip I paid $13. In terms of dollars most costs had risen 40 percent or more.

In fact, the inflation had gone so far in Switzerland that the Swiss franc was doing a poorer job of buying in Switzerland than the U.S. dollar was doing in America. The counterpart of an American secretary earning $800 a month would earn a comparable wage in Swiss francs related to dollars. However those same wages would give the stenographer in Switzerland a far lower living standard than she would enjoy in America.

Costs are proportionately high also in Germany, where the mark has been touted as the world's strongest currency. Gasoline costs $1.60 to $1.80 a gallon. It costs $40 to install a telephone. The rental is $10 a month, and then you must pay an additional fee for each and every phone call.

As the monetary crisis deepened on the world, the dollar, being the flagship of all money, took the greatest beating from a reputational standpoint. Hordes of dollar holders have rushed during the past years to change their dollars into the stronger Swiss, German, even Belgian and Dutch currencies; yes, even Japanese currency. As the dollar continued to sink against those currencies, more holders of dollars became alarmed and changed more dollars into those currencies—still further worsening the situation. Actually, the more dollars that are turned into those currencies, the less the currencies become worth in comparison with the dollar. If we take x as the value of the money supply in Switzerland, and we double the number of francs, we come up with half-value for a franc. At the same time, if we take y as the value of all of the money supply of the United States, and we cut this in half because we transfer half of the money into other currencies, we have doubled the value and the purchasing power of the American dollar in America.

The above is merely illustrative, of course. I use it to press home a point:

In the age of floating exchange rates (that is where no currency is fixed in value against another) the currencies of the world are like stocks on the stock market. They are subject to fashion, belief, psychology, swings. These swings are not always sensible—any more than the swings in the stock market are always sensible. Today it is very dangerous to adopt a slogan, a belief, or a formula. Just as it was dangerous to say the stock market is a hedge against inflation, so now it is dangerous to say that this currency or that is better and will remain better than the other currency.

In my trip in 1975 I came to the conclusion that too many people had been buying Swiss francs and German marks—in other words, it had been overdone. In still other words, the dollar had been oversold, it no longer was wise to change dollars into those other currencies. The dollar was at about 2.4 Swiss francs. It's not many years ago when it was worth four Swiss francs.

That was not to say that because the process had been overdone it would not be still further overdone. But basically, as things stood in the spring of 1975, it seemed to me that the dollar, sooner or later, ought to appreciate against the currencies that had risen so far above it—and for the simple reason that it was doing a better job as money in the United States than those currencies were doing in their native countries.

But, with the variable exchange rates in force all over the world, what can be said today may not be said with any confidence tomorrow. By the time this book is in your hands the situation could have changed again.

However, the above suffices as an explanation of why currencies swing against one another, and that nowadays currency prices are much like stock market prices. They are subject to change and they are subject to psychology. A currency that may be a haven today may be the opposite tomorrow.

It means that the foundation of all the moneys of the world is shifting daily, like sands on the desert.

This condition will remain in force until world money is stabilized; that is to say, until the monetary crisis has been resolved.

It is not encouraging but I can't help portraying it here in all its nakedness. For it is the stark truth.

THE ENERGY CRISIS

As if we didn't have enough on our minds already, we must now have a crisis on energy. For the United States this is less serious than for almost any other country. The United States still produces about 80 percent of its energy. However, the production is falling and the dependency of the United States will grow.

The United States, however, is such a heavy consumer of energy that even though it only has to import a fraction of its needs, its balance of payments deficits, because of its imports, nevertheless are greater than those of any other country. It soon may cost the United States $20 billion a year for its imports of oil. Only a couple of years ago that bill was $5 billion. Unless the United States is going to cut down drastically on its consumption of energy, it will have to issue still more masses of dollars, which will then, in time, be transformed into other currencies, causing a reflection of inflation in all the countries to which it flees.

Meanwhile, the Arab countries have been making big noises about not accepting American dollars. Kuwait said it wanted to be paid in Swiss francs. But, from the above section on currencies, how could Switzerland ever issue enough Swiss francs to finance the oil bills in the world? Impossible.

Other countries suggested the German mark. The answer is essentially the same.

There was a suggestion that commodities be tied together in an index and that the price of oil be tied to this index, so that, when all commodities in total came down, the price of oil would come down; and when all the commodities in total went up, the price of oil would go up. This was a fairly sensible suggestion by Iran, but it will take an unusual amount of international agreement to bring it to pass.

Then there was the suggestion to price oil by the basket of currencies, which is really the SDR. Today they figure the values of several currencies and give a weight to each one, and they call that the SDR. Then if the dollar goes down against the other currencies, they say the dollar has depreciated against the SDR.

Of course the SDR is nothing but a doughnut hole in the first place with a quite arbitrarily specified diameter.

The energy crisis is no joke and may be the world's most serious problem.

Thousands of pages have been written on it, and I have written scores of pages myself. I think a lot of words are unnecessary; the energy crisis was very well summed up by Secretary Kissinger in an address of November 14, 1974. Here is a part of that address, outlining the problem:

> The economic facts are stark. By 1973, worldwide industrial expansion was outstripping energy supply; the threat of shortages was already real. Then without warning, we were faced first with a political embargo, followed quickly by massive increases in the price of oil. In the course of a single year the price of the world's most strategic commodity was raised 400% The impact has been drastic and global.
>
> The industrial nations now face a collective payments deficit of $40,000,000,000, the largest in history, and beyond the experience or capacity of our financial institutions. We suffer simultaneously a slowdown of production and a speed-up of an inflation that was already straining the ability of governments to control.
>
> The nations of the developing world face a collective yearly deficit of $20,000,000,000, over half of which is due to increases in oil prices. The rise in energy costs in fact roughly equals the total flow of external aid. In other words, the new oil bill threatens hopes for progress and advancement and renders problematical the ability to finance even basic human needs such as food.

The oil producers now enjoy a surplus of $60,000,000,000, far beyond their payments or development needs and manifestly more than they can invest. Enormous unabsorbed surplus revenues now jeopardize the very functioning of the international monetary system.

Yet this is only the first year of inflated oil prices. The full brunt of the petrodollar flood is yet to come. If current economic trends continue, we face further and mounting worldwide shortages, unemployment, poverty, and hunger. No nation, east or west, north or south, consumer or producer, will be spared the consequences.

An economic crisis of such magnitude would inevitably produce dangerous political consequences. Mounting inflation and recession—brought on by remote decisions over which consumers have no influence—will fuel the frustration of all whose hopes for economic progress are suddenly and cruelly rebuffed. This is fertile ground for social conflict and political turmoil. Moderate governments and moderate solutions will be under severe attack. Democratic societies could become vulnerable to extremist pressures from right and left to a degree not experienced since the '20s and '30s. The great achievements of this generation in preserving our institutions and constructing an international order will be imperiled.

Mr. Kissinger's answer to this great problem is, of course, world cooperation. I have found cooperation, in my lifetime of observation to date, to be a very flimsy proposition. In the end, it seems, issues are always settled not by cooperation, but by force. When all the chips are down, when all the arguments have been exhausted, when all the right things have been said, when all the worthy motives have been mouthed —when the crunch comes, the strongest man makes the decision.

Additionally complicating the energy crisis, we have the Israeli-Arab conflict. This is the hotbed of war. These parties are so divergent, and their claims are so just on both sides, that compromise cannot be counted upon. In the end, the Arab-Israeli dispute will not be settled except by force.

It can only be hoped that the conflict would be contained within the area of the Middle East. The danger to mankind is that the United States and Russia might be unwillingly drawn into such uncompromising positions that they would come to blows with each other. The results are so horrible to contemplate that one must maintain hope that this will never come to pass.

There is a theory that was printed by the *Washington Observer Newsletter* that Secretary Kissinger made a deal with Brezhnev in which the Russians agreed to keep hands off the Middle East if the United States would agree to keep hands off while Russia went in and destroyed the nuclear capability of China.

We common people cannot hope to understand, much less to foresee, what will happen on the international political and military scene. Things have gone so far now that the best anyone can hope to do is to protect himself and his family to the greatest extent possible.

What can be said for certain is that the days of cheap and abundant energy are gone. Cheap and abundant energy was the secret of the great growth of the United States. It was the secret of the most advanced living standard in the world. The consequence of falling supplies at home is the end of the growth of this living standard and, temporarily at least, some shrinkage.

There is a fairly substantial reason to hope that by the year 2000 other sources of energy will have been developed by an advancing technology. That is small comfort to people who are now in their fifties or sixties. You simply must be prepared for a reduction in the available energy you can use. And that is not for a month or a year; that is for the rest of your life.

The energy crisis is real. It is not a crisis because there isn't enough oil in the world. It is a crisis because of the location of the oil.

Complicating the crisis is the fact that the producers of the oil cannot count on the currency they receive to hold its value.

Solve the monetary crisis and you solve the currency crisis. Solve the currency crisis and the worst of the energy crisis will have disappeared.

You see how they are all linked together.

THE STOCK MARKET AND BONDS

We have already dealt at length with the stock market. Bonds are a related subject.

When you buy a bond you lend your money. You expect an income until a certain date, at which time your money will be returned. To date the money has always been returned. Of course, half of the tomatoes you have received back have been rotten, so that you have only received half, or at least some part, of the amount of money you originally invested. You have definitely been robbed. But that is not the worst. At least you have received something. The question is whether you will get anything at all in the future. You have seen, from the reading of this book, the enormous structure of credit, and I would refer you again to page 00 showing the growth of the U.S. debt. You must have concluded that these debts can never be paid off. If you were to examine the British debt and the Italian debt, and so on, you would have to decide that they too could not be paid off. You must admit that no effort is being made to pay them off. You must admit that they are mounting constantly by enormous interest compounding steadily. You must admit that, even if the debts weren't increased except through interest, they would, by themselves, increase to astronomical and impossible proportions to the point where confidence is completely lost.

New York City is a dress rehearsal for what will happen to the credit of other city, state, and national treasuries.

This book was written almost in its entirety before there was any sign of the New York bankruptcy. The stark reality, which opened its jaws to swallow New York, comes as a vindication of the monetary *truth* of the preceding chapters. It shows that there is a limit to debt.

In the spring of 1975, people were still happily purchasing New York bonds. Who dreamt that $100 would ever decline to $35, and maybe a complete goose egg?

But the facts were there for the person who took the trouble to look at them. And they haven't changed any. Just substitute the U.S. for NYC—and there's your scenario for tomorrow. New York couldn't meet its current expenses, so how could one expect it ever to pay anything back? It had become a pattern. The interest on the debt threatened to become larger each year than the budget used to be.

New York proves there is a point at which investors lose confidence. When that happens it is *precipitation without warning.* (see chapter 1) It comes in a hurry.

It ought to have been an education to the American public to watch on TV the grim facts of New York—how large sections of the populace were threatening to bring out guns if they weren't properly fed. And how were they to be fed? How were the cops to be paid? How was law and order to be maintained? How was *chaos* to be avoided?

Sooner or later reality arrives.

Whatever the answer in New York, the spectacle will not go unheeded by prudent investors. It's all well and good to say it can't be allowed to happen. But who is going to put up the money to keep a spendthrift and delinquent debtor going?

A bail-out by the U.S. government is the beginning of the assumption of responsibility for every spendthrift municipality, city, and state. So the entire population again has to pay for mismanagement over which they had no control—and without their consent. But when enough get on the dole—who is left to do the paying?

The next casualty just might be New York State. The intolerable debt structure threatens to envelop ever-increasing masses to be held up by ever-declining masses, until the country is overbalanced by dependent masses.

Who will bail out the U.S. government? But just as in the case of New York City, the unmanageable debt is there; and it is growing every year. And it will never in this world be paid back.

New York proves that there is a point at which confidence disappears, and bonds can no longer be turned over. The principle is the same for a city, or a national government. The fundamentals are not altered by the size of the bankrupt.

Having admitted all this, you must admit that sooner or later all debts will have to be liquidated.

If the debts are liquidated by the method of inflation, it means that the bonds you buy will, of course, be sorely depreciated before you ever realize on them. Depending upon the degree of inflation (usually it ends in runaway inflation until it is stopped by deflation), you will get a lesser amount from the investment than you put in. This lesser amount may drop almost to zero if the scenario is a continuing inflation. If the solution to the great debt of the world is through runaway inflation destroying the value of money, your bonds are a rotten investment.

If, on the other hand, the scenario is deflation—if the credit structure is to fall through bankruptcies just wiping out the money supply, then the chances are that most classes of bonds will be vulnerable to that solution. That means you would get nothing for your bonds. They would simply be defaulted.

Either way you look at it, over the long run bonds must be a disaster.

You are advised to get out of bonds completely. With bonds there is no way you can win. What has been said for bonds can also be said for lending money to corporations or, for that matter, almost to anybody. The lender today ends up a sucker.

Normally, in cases of deflation, the lender makes out very well, because the money he is paid back buys much more than the money he lent. That's all well and good if the man to whom he lent it pays him back; that is, if the man doesn't go bankrupt. Today the credit structure in the world is so bad that it's hard to find any institution or government that can be counted upon to remain solvent. It's very bad to lend. Because we are not sure whether the credit structure will be liquidated by deflation or inflation—it is also very bad to borrow. If the crisis ends in deflation (as it surely will in time) then you will owe money that is worth much more than it was when you borrowed it.

So the debt situation, the bond situation, and the stock market situation, because of the liquidity crisis approaching, are all very bad. You should stay strictly away from them.

In the forefront of the bankruptcies would be the banks, where deposits up to $40,000 are covered by about one percent of federal insurance, and larger deposits by nothing at all.

THE LABOR CRISIS

This subject has not been dealt with so far in this book because it is quite complicated, and it is not necessarily intermixed with monetary affairs. Nevertheless it is a crisis that has helped to produce the vast inflation, and that—once inflation has got rolling—continues to aggravate it to the point where corporations find themselves helpless against further wage increases—beyond productivity—and the politicians do not have the nerve to stop issuing the necessary additional money.

Even in stable times, the strong and militant labor unions tend to demand wage increases beyond any increase in productivity. The moment such extra money is injected into the monetary stream we have an element of inflation. That is clear if, again, we go back to the state of Freedonia and find that a certain group is getting money beyond what it is producing. It is watering the money supply. Which brings us back to the foundation of all society, "Thou shall not steal."

If the labor union of Freedonia demands money in excess of what it produces, diluting the value of all other people's money, then it has taken from the people. They have suffered the loss—just as if the money had been counterfeited.

Every time a group of people get more money than their production justifies, the other members of the public pay the bill. They don't realize it, of course, until the situation becomes serious.

So, strong labor unions can be withstood for quite a long time if inflation is modest. The big trouble is that, once inflation gets going, the demands of the labor unions become evermore excessive—adding to the inflationary spiral. Those workers who do not have unions and who are unable to enforce their demands, and all other people on fixed incomes, pay the bill for the excessive demands of the strong labor unions.

By the 1960s, and particularly in the '70s, the strong unions had become monopolies. Policemen would strike, threatening the loss of law and order if their demands were not met. Firemen would strike, leaving the population open to the danger of holocausts. This, of course, was pure blackmail. But there was no possibility of negotiation with these unions if they wanted to hold out.

They had become monopolies through the device of the *closed shop*.

With the beginning of the seventies, negotiations with labor unions became a joke. You didn't negotiate. You just gave them what they wanted—or very close to it.

So a company like General Motors, or U.S. Steel, would agree to a large rate increase. During the sixties they merely tacked this on to the price of the goods and their profits remained the same—or were even more. They cared very little.

However in the seventies, as purchasing power began to shrink, the corporations were running into a wall on the other side. As long as they had room to retreat, they could yield to the labor unions. But when they hit the wall of buyer resistance, they were finding difficulty in selling their products. Now the demands of the labor unions were beginning to come out of profits—not out of additional costs. As profits shrank, the confidence in the ability of the companies to pay dividends undermined the value of their shares.

In 1975 Consolidated Edison shocked the whole investment world by dropping its dividend. When a utility could no longer pay—where was an equity that could be counted upon for an income? The flagship of all equities was sinking.

But the workers for utility companies had an even more powerful blackmail weapon than any other group. If they quit, the country would be crippled.

Of course inflation could have been stopped by the government, in any case, if it had simply refused to increase the money supply. That should have happened long ago in the sixties. Then the corporations, unable to sell their products, would have had to close down some of their factories. The workers would find themselves without work, and would turn against their leaders who had demanded the excessive increases.

But that didn't happen. The Federal Reserve continued to issue whatever money was necessary. There was no brake anywhere on the demands of the labor unions—and therefore on prices—and therefore on the growing inflation.

By 1973 inflation had gone so far as to justify many of the demands of the labor unions. But it was a sickness that had been generated to a large extent by themselves. Nevertheless, we had now reached a stage where inflation was feeding upon itself, and there was really no way to stop it—except *to stop issuing more money*. The government would absolutely have to stop increasing the money supply unless it was matched by increased productivity.

Of course no government *had* the courage, and no government *will have* the courage to do such a thing. Once again, increasing inflation becomes inevitable until it smashes itself. When it does, the labor unions will be smashed with it.

That is why declining inflation is not even a possibility. When the politicians talk about reducing inflation they are just whistling "Dixie." Once inflation is feeding on itself, there is no remedy except to kill the beast. Like a dandelion stimulated with a chemical growth-stimulant, it must grow until it dies.

So, once again, inflation must continue until eventually it demands such enormous issues of money that the money either becomes worthless or the social order is hit by mountains of bankruptcies that will wipe out the greatest portion of the money supply. In either case you end with a terrible deflation and depression.

Thus organized labor has brought upon itself a crisis that will help to destroy the social order that supports it and that will then have to end with a dictatorship of either the left or the right. The only hope that such a dictatorship could be avoided would be if the deflation would set in at once, rocking corporations from one end of the country to the other and throwing millions out of work.

Unfortunately, those are the hard and unalterable facts.

THE FOOD CRISIS

We haven't said much about this, and not much will be said, because you can find it in many popular magazines. But there are a few stark facts that need to be brought to your attention. There are now some millions on the verge of starvation, and many millions are already starving. Huge volumes of food must be provided if these people are to be kept alive. There are now a few less than four billion in the world, and the expectations are that we will be up to nearly seven billion by the year 2000. We have been told that technology will perform the miracle of feeding all.

Well, technology doesn't have a very good record in that respect. We have been applying ever more and more technology. When I was a boy we plowed the land with a single-furrow plow and, later on, when I was a youth, with three furrows and ten horses. At first we could cut 14 inches of sod, and then we could cut 42.

Today they cut it up in swaths more like 40 feet than 40 inches. Monstrous machines pull huge earth-tilling equipment so that one man today produces the wheat that was produced by scores of men 50 years ago.

But we have not kept up with the food demand of the world. Population has grown faster than production in spite of the constant stimulation of advanced technology. Nearly all the available land is under cultivation.

And this is going to continue. We might as well face the fact that it will be utterly impossible to feed the growing multitudes of human beings on this planet. Since most of the planet is too unsophisticated to practice birth control, there is not much chance that the population will stop growing. Even if they began to practice birth control now, and there was zero increase, the present youth of the world would still bring a food crisis upon us.

The world must face inevitable mass starvation.

The question is, where will this starvation take place? The advanced industrial countries have big pulpits from which the politicians preach of the necessity of sharing with the rest of the world. To bring this down to a practical application, you could then expect the following situation. The citizens of the United States would say: whereas today we consume

500 pounds of grain, and 100 pounds of meat, and 50 pounds of sugar, we know that many people in the world have hardly any of these foods; therefore if we are Christians, we must then, next year, eat only 100 pounds of grain, ten pounds of meat, and two pounds of sugar. We shall have a referendum on this, and we shall vote to dispose of our food supply in this manner—because, after all, we are Christians and we are generous people.

It wouldn't come to pass *exactly* that way, but it would happen in reality *just about* that way.

Politicians who intended to make this kind of a division would be voted out of office. Politicians who voted to retain the food supply for the United States would be retained.

If you wish to be a realist you cannot avoid the logic and the truth.

Then how are the increasing hundreds of millions to be fed? Not by technology. Not by the advanced countries. Not at all.

Then comes a very important moral question facing a hard-headed decision. The question is this:

If the increasing hordes cannot be fed, is it wise, or even humane to provide the present hordes with just enough food to allow them to reproduce new hordes facing certain starvation?

Are you doing them a favor by teasing them along at a bare subsistence level by virtue of a program that you know you cannot continue?

What can the developing countries do about it as their populations increase? What can the industrial countries do about it? And what will happen to the leaders of the industrial countries that do something about it to the point where it begins to pinch their own populations?

And how can anything be done as long as world money remains in its present chaotic condition, moving toward a state of collapse?

And the next and final question is: what can you do about it?

28

WHAT CAN YOU DO ABOUT IT?

The first thing you can do about it is to recognize that you can do nothing more than look after yourself and yours. You will be doing society a favor if you do that. If there are enough people who can remain healthy and sufficient, there is still a chance that able leadership will emerge.

In doing so, the first and most important question you must consider is whether we are faced with another wave of inflation, or whether, indeed, deflation is now on its way. These answers call for completely opposite reactions.

If there is going to be another wave of inflation, you should load up with debt and then pay off with cheaper dollars. If, on the other hand, we are now heading into deflation, you should get rid of every dollar of debt and hold cash and hard-core assets.

Another wave of inflation presumes the Fed has the will and, what is more important, the *ability* to inject new billions into the money stream.

An increase of the money supply depends mainly upon borrowing. Unless the psychology of the American consumer can be turned around, consumers will not start new borrowing that will create more new money. Until consumers start to demand more and buy more, business will not expand more. Therefore business will not borrow more. Therefore, in spite of the great increase in the money supply caused by the Federal deficits, the total money supply will continue to shrink. As it shrinks it will bring about bankruptcies, and these bankruptcies will cause others, which will end in a great domino display of deflation. The destruction of money will far outpace the manufacture of money by the Fed, and we shall be plunged into the worst depression in the history of the world.

I had one ally in this view in 1975, and that was John Exter, formerly Governor of the Bank of Ceylon and Executive Vice President of the First National City Bank, and formerly of the Federal Reserve Board. Mr. Exter thought that the Fed would not be able to meet the wave of bankruptcies because of the inextricable web of interwoven debt. Simply stated, the banks owe money internationally. Banks in England owe money to American banks; American banks owe money to Swiss banks; Swiss banks owe to other banks. There is over $130 billion in the Eurodollar market—that is, money in the form of dollars outside the United States. If the Central Bank of Italy could not support its own banks, then these banks would not be able to pay loans that might be coming due, for instance to Chase Manhattan Bank—and so on, and so on.

It is a very complicated argument. The mass of economists and political leaders and bankers were expecting a huge new wave of inflation. Some were expecting runaway inflation of the type Germany once had.

Actually, I don't think you have to answer the question. All are agreed that even if there is another wave of inflation, in the end we will have the worst deflation we have ever experienced.

In the United States such a deflation would result in a terrible depression and would, in my view, trigger social violence unprecedented in civilized history.

Jacques Rueff warned long ago that the social order itself was at stake unless the monetary mess could be straightened out. It has not been straightened out, and I believe the social order is in danger of disintegration.

Out of such chaos usually arises a dictatorship. In the process there is much suffering.

In the process there would be much lawlessness and a breakdown of law and order.

In this event you would need to be prepared for the worst. You would need money that would be acceptable anywhere.

For those who have small means the money of last resort would be United States silver coinage. This can be bought through coin dealers.

However it may best be bought through the New York Mercantile Exchange in bags that have a nominal face value of a thousand dollars, but which, in 1975 were running somewhere between $3,000 and $3,400 per bag. Several people could chip in together and buy a futures contract of a bag of silver coins of the current month. They could then take delivery of that bag. When they got it home they could divide it among them. Large commissions should not be paid for the purchase of silver coins to coin dealers.

If you have somewhat better means you should have the silver coinage for emergency spending, but you should also have gold coinage. Here a tremendous amount of wealth can be stored in a very small space. A normal safety deposit box could store scores of thousands of dollars. The gold coins could be buried. So could the silver coins be buried.

I have read that when Peron fled Argentina for Spain he took his fortune in millions upon millions of dollars in gold coins—not bars, coins.

In the event of deflation, cash itself would be a very good thing to hold. You will have to watch the developments, and if the present budget deficits do not result in growing inflation, you can be pretty sure we are headed on the road to deflation. Cash then becomes a very good holding. But be careful where you keep it.

In the deflation that would develop would come the bankruptcies of many banks. It seems that the Federal Reserve would stand behind the first banks. But the question I have asked, without getting a satisfactory answer, is this: What happens when people, terrorized by the failure of a major bank supported only in the nick of time by the Federal Reserve, get scared that the Federal Reserve might not back the next failure. Wouldn't they draw out their money in massive amounts, causing a run on all banks? The Federal Deposit Insurance fund for banks for deposits up to $40,000 would look after about one percent of the bank accounts of under $40,000. In other words, the insurance fund is almost as likely to go broke as a major bank itself.

Even a greater danger, as pointed out by John Exter, might be the large holders of funds in banks—in other words, banks. If a large bank were in danger, it is quite possible that the other banks holding deposits in that bank would withdraw their funds, as would the big holders of Certificates of Deposits in the hundreds of thousands of dollars. What you would have when the deflation actually arrives would be a debacle and a destruction of money unimaginable.

So if you have cash, certainly keep a close eye on the situation, and, if you see danger developing—not necessarily just in the United States, but with large banks in other countries—you ought to be withdrawing that cash and changing it either to gold or silver, or actually holding it in greenback form in your own possession or in well-guarded safety deposit boxes.

I am reproducing here a concept devised by John Exter but drawn by me that shows you the hard core of the money pyramid—the last-ditch-stand of hard money when everything else goes to pieces. At the top you have the instruments of credit and the stocks, and then the bonds, and then the treasury bills and the cash, and at last the silver and the gold.

If and when worst comes to worst, you must dig to the bottom of this pyramid for utter security. As these words are written, the time has not yet come—but each man must watch the events. With the understanding that you have derived from this book you should be able to read the events and project appropriate action.

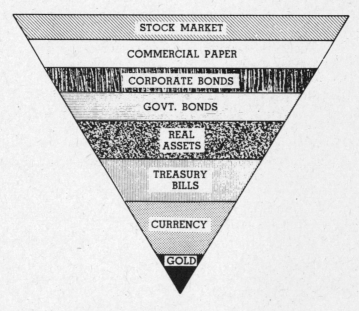

The Upside-Down Pyramid of Credit
The above graph is qualitative and illustrative only and
represents the author's concept of safety.

You should be fairly well off with the top silver stocks in the United States. You can find out from your broker which stocks these are. Buy only the leaders with established reserves and established earnings. Don't take chances on any speculation over and above the price of silver itself.

You should, of course, stay completely away from the industrial stocks and, in general, the stock market, and you ought to liquidate your bonds because eventually this credit pyramid must collapse.

You should watch the South African situation with an eye on the Middle East and the possibility of an outbreak of war over energy, or a war simply between Israel and the Arab states that would be the same as a war over energy.

South Africa itself seems to be politically quite stable. Nevertheless, we cannot overlook the fact that the perimeters have been more than ever closely drawn. Angola, Mozambique, and now Rhodesia have either been brought under black rulership or are close to it. It would seem as if the noose is drawing closer around South Africa. There is no reason at this time for alarm, but in the long range, South African gold stocks are losing their attractiveness.

For the intermediate term, note that the medium and long-life mines are good revenue producers. Their reserves are proven and known. Their share price is dependent on the price of gold. Gold itself caught up with prices in general in 1974, and then went a little too far. Nevertheless, four to five times the old $35 price ($140—$180) is entirely reasonable as a stable range of considerable duration—as long as other prices stay in that range.

Your broker can roughly calculate what earnings ought to be at a specific time for an established mine. (Ten times dividend is a reasonable hold for medium and long-life gold mines.)

Of course, in the case of war, there could be a panic about South Africa under certain conditions. What I am saying is that if world turmoil increases, the stocks of every kind are less safe than the metal.

As I noted in "The Year of the Metals," a newsletter I produced in early 1975—the ultimate safety lies with the metals. The leading metals for ultimate safety are gold and silver. For large wealth one needs to go to gold; for small wealth one can do best with silver and, perhaps, a small amount of gold coins.

Under one set of circumstances, described above, cash may be king. You have to be on the alert for this: if deflation appears to be deepening, go more and more into cash—especially greenbacks that you keep in your own possession—and U.S. short-term treasuries which can be quickly converted to cash. These short-terms are the safest thing short of cash in your own possession.

Additionally, one must be prepared for unrest. In certain earlier chapters, I have given suggestions as to what should be done. Every man must make his own plans according to his own circumstances. He must watch the trend of events.

On the basis of what you have now digested you must use your own intelligence, foresight, and initiative to weather the storm as it approaches.

Consider it a storm, as described in the following short chapter.

29

THE STORM

If we have succeeded in understanding the basic nature of money, the history of inflation, the nature of inflation, the inexorable Frankenstein-ian advance of inflation once it has been firmly established—if we have succeeded in obtaining a rock-bottom comprehension of the natural forces that propel human nature, then by now we must have arrived at the conclusion that there can be but one end to the present worldwide inflation. That is a collapse of the value of money. Such a collapse usually comes in the form of an exponential curve, rising rather swiftly to a crescendo near the end. We do not know exactly where we stand on this graph today, and there is no means by which we can predict the time of the final flourish.

But it is not always necessary to predict time. It is often enough for us merely to know that a thing will happen, without exactly knowing when. Consider this:

THE STORM

Among my earliest memories are memories of THE STORM. It was a small frame house of perhaps 500 square feet and it sat alone (so it seemed to me) on a vast and endless plain. Far beyond my known horizons lay a town. And in that town you could—if you had money—buy coal and lamp oil, sugar, even some preserves. The town was a reality only when the weather was right. It was a day's journey. We were as far from the town, in time, as Los Angeles from London.

When the deep winter set it, when the storms came, the town might as well have been London. Anything you needed from the town must have been laid in store long before THE STORM. You knew the storm would come. And you took it for granted. And you laid in the store of goods, with such resources of money as you had.

Long, long before any sign of snow we were getting ready for THE STORM. The early frosts brought us to our knees, plucking potatoes from the soil, pouring buckets of red spuds into sacks, and storing these in the dark cellar. There was canning of beans and beets; and even peaches—if we could afford them from the town. As the frosty mornings moved in, and long before the daylight, I could hear the rattle of the wagon as my father set out for the mine to lay in the winter's store of coal.

When it was all done, it was a pretty safe feeling. There was oil for the lamps, sacks of flour and sugar, dried prunes and raisins. The chicken house had been thatched; the hens were comfortable on the straw. The cows were in the nearby pasture. The barn was ready. When it was all done we read by the evening lamp. And we didn't worry. We knew THE STORM would come. We didn't have to know *what day*. And we didn't worry.

When, at length, the sky grew black in mid-afternoon and the wind began to whistle round the eaves and the temperature started to drop we were almost glad. The snow fell. The winds howled. The darkness settled, and the drifts piled high. So high, sometimes, that a boy could not see over them. Even when it went to 20 degrees below, 40 degrees below, and the chill factor stood at 90 degrees so that three minutes would freeze your nose off, we made our quick trips, as necessary, to the well and the barn. The warm milk was in the pails. The pot-bellied stove glowed its heat. And as the storm increased in fury, my father would say: "Let her come. We were here first." He would say it on the third day, and if need be, say it on the tenth day: "Let her come. We were here first."

The storm always blew out. And the sun shone again. And eventually there was spring.

Had we not known the storm was coming, of course, we should have perished.

I feel very strongly that we have had all the signals we could ask for in predicting the monetary and economic storm. Already the skies in the north are black, and the winds are rising. The temperature is dropping. This may be a preliminary storm, or it might be THE BIG ONE. On the farm we didn't worry if the storm came a little later than we expected. The important thing was to be ready for it. It came when it came. Why should we wish it before it came? Or why should we conclude that because it had not yet arrived, it would not happen at all?

We are now entering the period of winter. And if we are not ready for it, we are very stupid. If we are ready for it, we need not fret, nor hope that it will happen tomorrow, nor hope sooner or later; because we have no control. Our situation is simply this: To the best of our financial and economic ability we have stocked our cellar, boarded up our house, and we might as well relax. "Let her come. We were here first."

But I say to you, there is no question about what will happen. And it looks like an early winter. So fill up the lamp, get in some good books. Philosophically wait it out in a QUIET CORNER. You were here first!

The subject of this book has been The Coming Deflation. In order to establish and substantiate this title it has been necessary to go into many aspects of the monetary situation that are not directly involved with the current crisis, or the upcoming crisis. But it has been necessary to include all this if, intellectually, we are to understand why these crises took place.

In this book I have tried to make clear all of the facts that I believe are necessary to an acceptable and comprehensive understanding of world money, national money, prices and wages, controls, balance of payments, convertibility. These all have the aura of formidable mysteries when we read of them one by one in the press. Taken together here, I hope they come forth quite as simply as the stories of Hans Christian Andersen. They don't have the beauty, I admit, but I hope they have the truth.

And now we must touch on the most unpleasant possibility of all. That is virtual revolution in the United States.

This book is concerned with the end of an era. That means the end of an era of permissiveness, the end of an era of the spoilage of people, the end of an era of credit and waste, the end of an era of something for nothing, the end of an era to buy now and pay later, the end of an era of dependence on someone else.

Americans aged 40 years and younger have become so accustomed to the idea that the country owes them at least a living that the withdrawal of this presumed privilege could result in widespread rioting across the nation. Empty bellies produce inflamed minds. When it comes to considering the possibility of violent protest, it's difficult to project either the upper or the lower limits. The lower limits could be rioting throughout the large cities. The upper limits could be organized revolution.

In case there is rioting, do not join. Likewise do not join the marches or the protests. Crowds often become unexpectedly insane. Don't become members of the crowd. Stay at home, watch it on TV, and have a beer. Keep your children off the street in times of disquiet. It wouldn't do any harm to have a few games, and to use a little imagination now in projecting the interesting use of time that you may find on your hands. One good use for a little surplus cash would be a secondhand set of the *Encyclopaedia Britannica,* or some other good encyclopedia or reference books.

In preparation for the time that will inevitably fall upon us—sooner or later—every man must rely upon his own imagination, his own projection, and his own initiative.

If this book has helped you to understand what has happened to the United States, what is happening, and why it is happening, it will have served its purpose. You will then, of your own initiative, be able to come up with your own solutions particularly applicable to your personal conditions in THE STORM.

One thing is certain, you will see the collapse of this inflation and that will mean the end of the era you have known.

EPILOGUE

THE DAY THEY FLOATED THE ARK

Starring

Mr. Knowa	Mr. Whena
Mr. Doubta	Mr. Dumbo

While Knowa and his sons are hammering the last nails into the completed Ark, his neighbors gather around.

Mr. Whena: Friend Knowa, it is a beautiful morning. The birds are singing in the trees, the dust is blowing along the trail. I know you say there is going to be a great flood that will sweep us all away. Sometimes I half believe you. But when?

Mr. Knowa: I cannot tell you the day of the flood. I do not know whether it is tomorrow, next month, or next year. But I can tell you, if you do not build yourself a ship, you will surely drown. And you cannot build yourself a ship overnight.

Mr. Whena: Yes, but you have been saying for two years that there is going to be a flood. Several times you have scared me to death. But always the sun shone again, and it turned out to be no more than an ordinary rain.

I do believe that you had a vision and that there will be a flood. Meanwhile, others are reaping crops and making money. As long as the weather looks this good, I am not about to miss these profits to get ready YET for your flood.

Mr. Dumbo: The whole thing is silly. It is inconceivable that all this land should be covered by water. Has it ever happened before, Mr. Knowa? No, never. And since it has never happened before, it cannot happen now. And even if the Lord did say there was going to be a flood, I say the Lord is wrong. It cannot happen, because it would be such a disaster— the Lord couldn't let it happen.

Mr. Doubta: I do not agree with Mr. Dumbo, that because it never happened before, it can never happen. But I doubt that it will happen in our lifetime. At least I am sure that if such a flood is to come, the water will rise very gradually, and we will have plenty of time to see what is happening. In other words, the water will rise a little more each month and each year, and then we will all start to build our ships.

Mr. Knowa: Since I do not know exactly when the flood is coming, I cannot argue with you. But my position is this: I know the flood is coming. I know it takes me two years to build my ship. Thus I lose two years of crops. But, if at the end of that time the flood has not come, my ship is ready, and I shall return to growing crops. It costs me nothing because my ship is ready. You, on the other hand, will still have to take out two years from your crops to build your ships, and you run a risk that I do not run. Because you do not *know* that the flood will not come in six months.

So, if the flood comes in six months, my family and I and all our species will be saved—and you will all drown. You will have reaped this harvest in vain, because you will never get the chance to build your ships.

The difference between you and me is that you gamble, and I don't.

Mr. Whena: But I think you are an extremist. Before I am going to let my crop go, I must have a better idea as to when. I see these pretty nice profits right now, and last year I started my ship, and failed to fallow my land, and lost money because of you. And I do not intend to lose any more. When I *know when*, then I will go back to building my ship.

Mr. Dumbo: Every day it doesn't rain, the crowd laughs at you. Everyone knows that such a wild thing has never happened before, and we are therefore on very sound ground to doubt that it will happen at all.

(They all begin to laugh at Knowa, and Mr. Dumbo laughs the loudest.)

Mr. Knowa: Who laughs last laughs best.

That night the sky grew inky black, and the rain commenced to fall, first in sheets, then in a veritable deluge, 'til by morning all the water holes were filled, and the valleys were rushing torrents. And by afternoon the Ark began to lift, and Mr. Dumbo, Mr. Whena, Mr. Doubta, and their families were racing around frantically trying to build some small rafts. And they dropped their hammers in the water and could not find them, and their nails were washed away, and they began to swim, and the Ark rose. And a smile broke on Knowa's face, and as the Ark sailed away on the waves you could hear the roar of his laughter above the din of the torrents and the wind. Knowa was the last one heard to laugh.

And that is the origin of that wise old saying—"He who laughs last laughs best!"

(From *Myers' Finance & Energy,* April 8, 1971.)

INDEX